To Sharon,

I pray as you read this book,
you will gain knowledge and
understanding of God's Word.

May you grow in the things
of God as you remain steadfast
and obedient to God and His Word.

THE CALL OF
GOD

Keys to Understanding His Word

CORRENA R. BARZEY

LifeRich Publishing is a registered trademark of The Reader's Digest Association, Inc.

LifeRich Publishing books may be ordered through booksellers or by contacting:

LifeRich Publishing
1663 Liberty Drive
Bloomington, IN 47403
www.liferichpublishing.com
844-686-9607

Cover Design by Leilani Lindo

Scripture taken from the King James Version of the Bible.

ISBN: 978-1-4897-4093-9 (sc)
ISBN: 978-1-4897-4092-2 (hc)
ISBN: 978-1-4897-4094-6 (e)

Library of Congress Control Number: 2022905243

Print information available on the last page.

LifeRich Publishing rev. date: 03/17/2022

Contents

Acknowledgments

I first want to thank the Almighty God, for without His leading in my life, this book would not be possible. God, you deserve all the praise, glory, adoration, and thanks. For in every word in this book, one can feel His presence. Lives will be changed, and souls will be saved as people read and gain a clear understanding of God's Word.

There are some people I would like to acknowledge, for they have stood with me throughout my trials and tribulations by praying and encouraging me along my journey of pain and sufferings.

I would like to thank my children for being there for me; they were so supportive and comforting. They offered shoulders that I could rest my head on and cry, and they embraced me, thus giving me the strength to go on. I can't thank my children enough. Also, as I was writing this book, they were my listening ears. I read to them with excitement after I finished a chapter or even a paragraph, and I would then ask them, "How does this sound?" Every time, their response was the same: "Good, Mommy." They are my biggest fans and cheerleaders, and I love them; I thank God for them all.

Special thanks to my daughter Leilani Lindo for designing and drawing the cover picture for this book. Such a beautiful and creative masterpiece from a wonderful and talented child. May God continue to bless you abundantly.

Priscilla Adorm, my girl, you have a heart of gold, and I want to thank you for being there for me. Your prayers, love, and support are unmatched. I appreciate you as one of my children, and you will always be in my heart.

Sonia Dasent, thank you for your spiritual support, motherly care, and prayers. I truly appreciate them. You have been there with me through my heartbreak and my diagnosis with cancer, encouraging me spiritually, emotionally, and mentally. Thank you so much.

Petran Turnbull, you have been there with me for many years, encouraging me spiritually and emotionally throughout my ordeals. You are indeed a good friend. Thank you. I'm sincerely grateful to you and the women's ministry of your church for praying for me while I was battling cancer. Thank you all.

Lionel Lindo, you have been supportive in the writing of my first book, and when you found out I was sick, you prayed religiously for me. I just want to say thank you. I appreciate all that you have done for me and the children.

Sherine Lyte, although I just met you last year, you have been a source of strength to me. The love and support that you have shown to me is immeasurable, and I want to say thank you for your prayers and being there for me as a friend.

Lastly, I want to thank the Milton Keynes Church of Christ family for all their prayers.

Introduction

First and foremost, I want to give all praise and glory unto the Almighty God, for directing me to write this book. As I held the hard copy of my first book in my hands, the Holy Spirit spoke to me and told me to write this book. He then revealed to me the title and the topics on which to write about. At that time, I did not understand why God wanted me to write on those topics, but now I see why, as the world needs to turn back to Him. The coronavirus pandemic has humbled and crippled humanity, indicating that mankind is nothing without God and causing us to look unto God for His help.

We are living in the last days, and the time when the church, God's people, will be taken out of this world is fast approaching, as seen through the destruction, evil, wickedness, abominations, pandemics, and shortening of time as days, months, and years go by ever so quickly. We are told in the scriptures, "For as it was in the days of Noah, so also the coming of the Son of Man be" (Matthew 24: 37). God gave the people of Noah's time a period of 150 years to repent and turn to Him and the ark to save them, yet they refused and were surprised when the flood came.

Subsequently only Noah's family were saved. In today's time, God is sending warning after warning to mankind. He is sending His true preachers to warn the world so that they won't be caught off guard when He returns

This book is a reminder to the entire world that God is in control, sovereign. He wants to be God in the hearts, minds, bodies, and souls of mankind. He is desperately calling humanity back to Him, as He wants a relationship with them for He loves and cares for them. The world must never take God's patience for weakness; rather, know that He is only giving humanity a chance to turn to Him. The Lord is not slack concerning His promise, as some men count slackness; He is longsuffering to us, not willing that any should perish but that all should come to repentance (2 Peter 3:9).

ONE

The Call to Repentance

REPENTANCE IS A PROCESS THAT commences in the mind. It effects a change of attitude toward sin, which then brings a change of heart and triggers the desire to turn away from sin and return to God. It is choosing good over evil; it's abandoning all evil intentions, deeds, motives, and conduct and being radically changed.

Repentance is conscious, moral, and separate; it is a decision to forsake sin and seek the righteousness of Christ. It's a spiritual change that comes directly from God, which refers to God's relationship to humankind. The prophet Isaiah called the children of Israel to such change as he admonished them to cease from doing evil, to wash, and to make themselves clean before the presence of God. The apostle Peter, on the day of Pentecost, told the people to repent and be baptized in the name of Jesus Christ for the remission of sin (Acts 2:38; Deuteronomy 4:29–31; Isaiah 1:16).

Repentance begins with God's calling on our lives, as He opens our minds to the correct understanding and knowledge of His Word. It enters our hearts; it produces the desire to do good as we experience the grief of sin and evil.

Repentance involves these three principles:

- Emotion (our well-being)
- Mind (our intellect)
- Spirit (our will)

Repentance is motivated by our love for God, which in turn changes our minds, thoughts, and purpose as we abandon sin. It changes our inner selves as it affects our spiritual nature and our entire personality. Repentance affects us intellectually, emotionally, and voluntarily, as these involve our sin nature and the consciousness of personal guilt.

The mind is where a person understands the true nature of sin and the need to forsake it and turn to God. It is in the mind where the Word of God is effectual to sinners. Within the mind, after receiving the Word, a person turns away from sin, which brings about a change of thinking. The person views sin as sin and agrees with God's Word about sin. God's Word illuminates the power of the Holy Spirit to bring God's perspective of sin into our lives.

Emotion is important to repentance, as it involves godly sorrow for sins that we have committed. In demonstrating godly sorrow, we denounce self-satisfaction, arrogance, and pride. In their place, we put on humility and dependence on God's divine and saving grace, having genuine hatred toward sin. The apostle Paul tells us "that godly sorrow produces genuine repentance" (2 Corinthians 7:10).

The spirit empowers, directs, keeps us and alerts us to sin. It illuminates the areas in our lives that need change and impresses in hearts our need for the Savior, Jesus Christ. The Holy Spirit convicts and shows humankind the truth of God's Word, how wrong they are about sin, and God's justice and judgments (John 16:8).

The Holy Spirit operates in three areas:

- Judgment (convicts people of Satan's defeat at the cross)
- Righteousness (convicts people that Jesus Christ is the righteous Son of God)
- Sin (exposes sin and unbelief)

The Holy Spirit work of convicting humankind of sin, righteousness, and judgment will be manifested in all who have given their lives to Christ, are baptized in water, and have received the gift of the Holy Spirit.

Repentance is one of the most important spiritual principles in the scriptures. It is vital for anyone desiring to be near Christ and to live for Him. Repentance is an integral part of receiving eternal life, as Jesus taught in the beginning of His public ministry, for it is the condition of salvation that can only be found in God's divine grace and love. It involves constantly dethroning the pride and unworthiness that produce grief, practicing genuine humility, and having a strong spiritual desire for more of Christ. True repentance must precede forgiveness. Repentance is not a one-time occurrence; instead, it's an ongoing reassurance characterized in a follower of Christ's life.

Repentance is part of the foundation of the Christian faith and is at the heart of the kingdom message. Noah, the prophets, John the Baptist, Jesus, and Jesus's apostles all preached repentance, or to repent for the remissions of sins. It is a prerequisite for being born again. It's important to know that repentance, forgiveness of sins, and baptism are the prior conditions for receiving the gift of the Holy Spirit. Repentance is a key to growing spiritually in our relationship with Christ and to remaining faithful to Him.

God sent the prophets to prophesy on Him and to preach repentance. He sent His Son to die on the cross so that repentance and remission of sins would be preached in His name to all nations of the world. The scripture shows the consistency of God when it comes to repentance. From the beginning, He sent His servants, the prophets, with the same message and ended with His Son demonstrating the importance of repentance so that humankind can be saved. At the beginning, it was said, "Repent and turn from all your transgression," and at the ending, "Cast all your transgressions on Him and receive a new heart and spirit" (Jeremiah 25:4–5; Ezekiel 18:30–31).

Faith, repentance, and works are all interconnected. They all lead to a change of life behaviors and attitudes. Our repentance results in a change of mind, and faith in Jesus Christ leads to a new life in Him. Genuine repentance includes faith, and genuine faith includes repentance. Genuine repentance comes from an inner state that is firmly rooted and nurtured from within, thereby expressing itself through our outward works. The internal and external qualities of repentance cannot be separated, because our mindsets or attitudes influence our actions and behaviors.

Repentance is a choice that people make to align themselves with God, His Word, and His commands while being obedient to His will. Their hearts are being softened to the things of God. Thus, they receive clean hearts and no longer carry the burdens of sin and guilt as their love for God grows stronger, resulting in them receiving blessings from God. Turning away from our sinful lives toward righteous lives through faith and obedience to God will result in us having a change of mind and conduct, which will produce good fruits, for it will be proven in our actions. Genuine repentance will be accompanied by the fruits of righteousness (Matthew 3:8–10).

The importance of repentance is reflected in these statements:

- It changes one's mindset and behavior
- It is a command from God
- It is essential to the Great Commission
- It is linked to the kingdom of heaven
- It is necessary for salvation
- It is the main reason Jesus Christ came to earth

Through Adam, sin entered this world, and death was passed onto all humanity. This death refers to spiritual death—a separation from God—resulting in all humanity inheriting a sinful nature. Adam's sin was transmitted into the lives of humans. In today's world, we were all born with an impulse toward sin and evil. The only way humanity can escape this spiritual death is by the grace of God through repenting, having faith in Jesus Christ, and being saved (Ephesians 2:8).

In the Holy Scriptures, confessing sin and turning away from sin are the beginning of repentance, which is necessary for divine forgiveness from God. Those two actions are conscious decisions to turn to God and denounce sin, which is the free will God has given to everyone. We must admit our sins and seek forgiveness by reconciling ourselves to God and receiving purification from Him as He removes the guilt and the destruction of sin's power in our lives. Importantly, confession involves honesty and courage (1 John 1:9).

Jesus Christ called humankind to repent and to believe in Him. He includes the manifestation of God's power to rule the hearts and lives of all who repent and believe in the gospel. This manifestation comes with great spiritual power as we assert ourselves against the dominion of Satan, sin, and evil. The apostle Peter tells us that God is long-suffering toward those who come to repentance, describing God's patience in waiting. We (churchgoers and unbelievers alike) are called to repent and to exercise our faith in Christ (Mark 1:15; 2 Peter 3:9).

To repent is to change our minds from sin and recognize the need for the Savior, Jesus Christ. The initial step to repent is spiritual because it is God who leads us to repentance. This is the process of faith and obedience, for it's impossible to place our faith in Christ without a sincere change of mind about Jesus Christ and what He did on the cross. It is the starting point of a commitment to a new way of living that transforms our hearts and minds from carnal to spiritual. We have full understanding of the seriousness of sin and the desire to be forgiven. Faith, obedience, and repentance complement each other, as they are the steps to spiritual transformation and eternal life in Christ.

The scripture tells us "the goodness of God leads to repentance" (Romans 2:4) When we truly understand God and learn of His goodness, we then gravitate to the wonderful gift of salvation through His Son, Jesus Christ. God's forbearance continues to spare our lives, even when we sin against Him, for He is abounding in mercy. It's important to know that God does not make a person repent; it's our own free will to do so. Instead, He waits patiently; hence, we must look and live, believe and be saved, because God is a God of love, goodness, mercy, forbearance, and kindness.

One might ask, "Why we must repent?" We repent because we are all sinful. Our bodies are flesh and carnal-minded, which produces evil thoughts and actions that are not acceptable to God, and they break the law of God. Our flesh is susceptible to temptation because the flesh is weak; therefore, the mind and our existence crave the desires of sin. The apostle James tells us that sin is generated through our fleshly desires, and the apostle Paul tells us that nothing good dwells in the flesh. Satan takes advantage of our weakness and vulnerability to tempt and maneuver through the minds of humankind, thereby influencing the way we think (Romans 7:18; James 1:14-15).

Those who are in the flesh are unspiritual and are bearing fruits unto death because they still live after fleshly desires and are under the power of the sinful nature. Fleshly desires consist of "the lust of the flesh, the lust of the eyes and the pride of life" (1 John 2:16). These are the three basic categories of sin that Satan uses on mankind. The scripture tells us that because of sin everyone has fallen short of the glory of God. Sin is the transgression of God's law; therefore, sin is rebellion and a violation against God. Both the Old and New Testament define sin as an offense, disobedience to God—so basically sin is living apart from God and His law and separates us from Him (Romans 7:12–14; 1 John 3:4).

Satan is the originator of sin. He desires to be higher than God. After being thrown out of heaven, he brought sin into the world and to mankind. Sin begins in the mind when we allow evil to enter in, which eventually causes us to act on it and commit sin. Anything that is contrary to the will of God or does not express His holy character will bring suffering and punishment. Sin hates rather than loves. It doubts rather than trusts. It hurts rather than respects and helps. It destroys lives, for it is opposed to God's Law and principles.

How to repent

1. Acknowledge your sins to God
2. Admit that you are sinner and need of a savior
3. Ask God to forgive you of all your sins
4. Ask Jesus Christ to come into your life
5. Believe that God have forgiven you
6. Genuinely confess your sins to God

God called us to repent so that we could experience His love and purity and genuine worship toward Him, so that He can be our God. He wants us to be humble and honest, gain spiritual wisdom, build unity with others, and overcome sin and Satan's tactics. When we sin, we fail to measure up to the standards of God, because He has defined to us what is acceptable to Him and what is not; therefore, in sinning, we fall short of those standards and the fundamental principles

He has given us to live by. The good news is God has provided a way of escape so we can repent of our sins and turn to Him by faith through His Son, Jesus Christ.

All unrighteousness is sin. This includes our physical deeds and actions, our attitudes and motives for wrongdoing, and our unrighteous thinking. We must be careful not to violate our conscience and commit a sin of omission, which is basically not doing something that is right, sinning without knowing you've sinned. Jesus Christ gave two examples of sins of omission in the stories of the Good Samaritan and Lazarus and the rich man. These examples are to show us that it is sinful to avoid doing good. Overcoming sin is a lifelong process. It's important to recognize that whenever we sin, we need to seek God's forgiveness immediately. Therefore, we must avoid all sin and live productive, fruitful lives that would be in accordance with God's Word and our faith and acceptable to Him (James 4:17).

In recognizing that our sins bring grief to God, we ought to stop rationalizing our negative behaviors and attitudes and humble ourselves by showing remorse before Him, for remorse leads to godly sorrow. In the scripture, there are two sorrows mentioned: godly sorrow and worldly sorrow. Godly sorrow leads to repentance, turning away from sin to God, and receiving salvation. Worldly sorrow leads to unrepentance where the person feels self-pity and helplessness and often becomes sorry only for the consequences of his or her sins. Such sorrow results in eternal death and judgment. God declares that no sinful or unclean thing can inherit the kingdom of God. His forgiveness is available for all; therefore, repent and put away evil. Strive rather to do right and obey God's Word (2 Corinthians 7:10).

True repentance includes godly sorrow, honest confession of sins without excuses, and accepting responsibility for what we have done. Genuine repentance will be accompanied by fruits of righteousness, or what we accomplish for God after salvation. We must make it evident throughout our lives by being committed to following Christ, bearing good fruits, totally separating from our sinful nature, being obedient to His command, trusting in His promises, and using our gifts to build up the body of Christ (Matthew 3:8).

The benefits of genuine repentance include the following:

- Becoming a new creation
- Gaining godly and constructive fear
- Having a sense of discernment
- Releasing us from Satan's hold
- Removing fleshly desires
- Removing sin from our lives

Genuine repentance brings joy, peace, happiness, contentment, and fulfilment to the person who repented. In heaven, God and the angels rejoice whenever someone returns to God, for He wants everyone to hear and believe the gospel, as He does not take pleasure in anyone perishing. God's primary desire is to have mercy, not to execute His punishment on sinners, for He is a God who is moved with compassion for those who sincerely repent. Hence, the scripture tells us that "God desires for all to come to repentance, seek His forgiveness and have eternal life"; however, those who reject God's grace and salvation will be lost eternally; 2 Peter 3:9).

Repentance was the first message of Jesus Christ. John

the Baptist, the prophets, and the apostle Paul preached on it. Stephen's only message was of repentance. It was the apostles' first message after the ascension of Christ and the last message of Jesus Christ here on earth. Repentance was an important call throughout the Holy Scriptures, as it calls out sin for what it is. It demonstrates God's genuine love for His children, His patience, and His character. In modern society, repentance is ever so needed. The world is spiraling out of control and falling away from Christ, as it is in the hands of Satan. Mankind's pride, anger, lust, greed, and envy are exploding all over this world (Acts 3:19–21, 7:51–60).

A repentant person receives God's grace. His or her sins are forgiven, and he or she is delivered from the bondage of sin and born again, for God wipes the slate clean by throwing sin into the sea of forgetfulness. As we recognize our new identity in Christ, our lives are transformed by Him—His cleansing powers, His redemptive power, and our faith. Moreover, we are being controlled by the Holy Spirit, who now guides and leads us into all truth. We strive to live righteous lives, displaying the characteristics of Christ and the fruit of the spirit, thereby surrounding ourselves with the things of God; emulating Christ in our actions, motives, and behavior; being obedient to His commands; and always bringing glory to Him.

Regenerated, restored, refreshed, recovered, refocused, and released from Satan describes how a repentant person ought to be. This person should be wanting to know more about Christ and build a closer relationship by yearning and thirsting for Him. He or she should be studying, reading, meditating on the Word of God, praying, and seeking the presence of Christ in his or her life. The person should have a deep respect for Him and His holiness and form an intimate and deep love for Him. We must develop godly fear and earnestly desire to walk with God by renewing our minds in the things of God, growing in grace and the knowledge of Him, becoming a mature follower of Christ who is eager to apply holiness in our lives, and being separated from worldliness and carnality.

A genuinely repentant person dreads committing sins, and if for any reason, this person sins knowingly or unknowingly, daily, he or she would repent and have the fear of God in his or her life because the scripture tells us that there is no one righteous. Repentant people are living lives worthy of their calling by practicing godly characteristics, being completely humble and gentle, being patient, bearing with one another in love, and forbearing. They are unified in Christ, based on truth and righteousness. Thus, they make every effort not to compromise the foundational truth of God's Word and to be able to discern every spirit that does not acknowledge Jesus as savior.

God promised that He would be merciful to sinners who had repented, and He would not turn His face from them. His mercy is given to everyone to help alleviate the consequences of sin. His mercy is translated into hope for sinners, and it's a ubiquitous force that shapes all of humanity. It is a pervasive impetus for hope; hence, the scripture tells us, "The Lord is good to all, and His mercies are over all His works. Mercy and compassion are rooted in the very character of God, and the fullest expression of such mercy is found in the person and work of His Son,

Jesus Christ, the compassionate and incarnate God" (Psalm 145:9).

The mercy that God gives is His favor of compassion. His lovingkindness and His forgiveness are granted to the repentant as He is embracing, cleaning, and adopting them as members of His family. He reestablishes us as His sons and daughters. The scripture tells us that God is merciful and compassionate to those who repent. Throughout both the Old and New Testaments, God is constantly displaying mercy, first to the Israelites and then to all humanity through Jesus Christ. He is always waiting for us to open our hearts to Him, and it is only by accepting Christ into our lives that will we find enduring peace, joy, mercy, and abundant blessings (Luke 1:78–79).

In the scripture, we learn of God's judgment on the unrepentant. It teaches us that one's existence does not end at death but continues forever, either in the presence of God or in a place of eternal punishment called hell, where they will be condemned before God. The unrepentant are treasuring up the wrath of God against themselves on the day of judgment as He inflicts vengeance on those who disobey the gospel and reject Him. God's wrath is an expression of His holiness and righteousness. It is His personal anger, His unchanging response to sin and evil, which is provoked by wicked behaviors of individuals and unfaithfulness to Him (2 Thessalonians 2:7–10, Romans 2:5).

The judgment of the unrepentant and evildoers is certain. There is a place of punishment and separation from God with no end to its duration. It is the terrifying reality of continuous punishment, the place of "fire that never shall be quenched," of everlasting fire that is prepared for the devil, his angels, and the unrepentant. In this place will be wailing and gnashing of teeth, binding and darkness, torment and agony, and separation from heaven. God does not desire to send anyone to hell. Those who go there do so because they have resisted God's grace and rejected God's provision of salvation (Matthew 13:42).

In this present time, God's wrath toward the unrepentant is seen, as He gives them over to uncleanness and vile passion and in His bringing ruin and death to all who disobey Him. However, the beginning of God's wrath in the future will be in the tribulation period, where a complete retribution will occur at the end of this world, directed against impenitent wickedness. There will be great distress for the ungodly, a day of trouble and distress, a day of darkness and gloominess, and a day of reckoning for the unrepentant in this world.

Here are two reasons for God's abandonment of the unrepentant; it is to allow sin and its consequences to accelerate as part of His judgment upon sinners and to make them realize their need for Jesus Christ as savior. He also gives them a reprobate and depraved mind because of their hard and impenitent hearts, not wanting to acknowledge God; therefore, He leaves them to their own foolish thinking and ways. One important note is that God extends mercy to the wicked who repent, but to the unrepentant who despise Him, He has no pleasure in them, and they become subject to His wrath.

Repent from Sexual Immorality

Sexual immorality is a transgression of God's moral law. The seventh commandment encompasses all sexual sins. As a result, it places mankind outside of God's kingdom. Sexual immorality is translated in the scriptures as whoredom, fornication, and idolatry, which means to surrender one's sexual purity. It involves any type of sexual expression outside the boundaries of marriage. It is described to us as sexual sins that are a violation against a person's own body, especially those who are true followers of Christ, for the scripture tells us, "The body is the temple of Christ" (1 Corinthians 6:19). Their bodies are the personal dwelling place of the Holy Spirit, where He marks us as properties of God.

Sexual immorality includes adultery, which is any sexual activity or intercourse outside marriage, and fornication, which is any sexual sin, evil deed, or vice, including lustful thoughts and desires of the heart. These are abhorrent to God, more than any other sinful acts, as they desecrate the body and remove a person from union with Christ, thereby making his or her body a member of immorality and ungodliness. They also bring permanent and serious consequences and are abominable in God's sight; hence, the apostle Paul admonishes us to "flee fornication" by saying no to all ungodliness and worldly passions. Sexual sins are unique and dangerous because they involve two different individuals joining together as one. They always begin with impurities, such as passionate feelings, evil desires, and lust (1 Corinthians 6:18).

In today's society, people have redefined sexuality as a personal right that can be exercised the way an individual chooses; however, from the beginning of creation, when God created Adam and Eve, He joined them together as one in marriage, united physically and spiritually. Sexual activity outside marriage is a sin and is a violation of marriage. The scripture tells us, "Marriage is honourable in all and the bed undefiled" (Hebrews 13:4). This indicates that God has a high standard for His followers and has called us to be morally and sexually pure. Sexual purity is important to God. It allows Him to sanctify us and control our bodies so we can become more like Him. Sexual immorality jeopardizes the process of sanctification in our lives.

What causes sexual immorality?

- Exposure to sexual immorality
- Lack of God's Word
- Lack of prayer
- Pride
- Satan
- Sinful desires
- Wrong association

In the Holy Scriptures, when it speaks of sexual immorality, it always follows with a stern warning from God, as it is disobedient to Him, His commands, and His will. Sexual sins and all sins begin with temptation, as mankind allow their lust to dictate their choices, thus allowing their hearts to deceive and manipulate them into committing adultery and fornication. Those without the full knowledge of the Word of God are not protected, and they will always follow their sinful nature, being enticed by Satan the deceiver, who takes every advantage of such a privilege to destroy mankind (Mark 7:21).

Sexual immorality begins in the mind and manifests itself in the body as it controls our actions, emotions, and convictions. The eyes and ears are the gateway to the soul; therefore, it is vital that we guard our thoughts against any sexual acts. Protect your eyes and ears from engaging, watching, listening, or reading any sexually explicit things that will lead you to sin. Just as the eyes and ears are important to God for us to hear and read His Word, so too are they important to Satan because the eyes and ears are instruments of deception that he uses on humanity. The lust of the eyes started with Eve in the garden of Eden and continues to this present time.

Israel was portrayed in the Holy Scriptures as a wife to God, for it was God's chosen people, "the holy city," filled with all beauty and splendor; however, they began to trust in their riches and beauty instead of God. Israel was not spiritually faithful to God, as they not only committed spiritual adultery but also participated in sexual immorality, child sacrifice, and all kinds of religious abominations that God detested. For their unfaithfulness to God, He used the nations they followed and committed adultery with to punish and bring devastating destruction to Israel for their disobedience to Him (Ezekiel 16).

In today's world, spiritual adultery is being committed by the churches and individuals who turn away from God and give themselves to sinful pleasure, lust, and worldly values rather than God. Society today says sexual intimacy among committed singles is acceptable, thus showing no regard for God's standard, even though God stipulates that any sexual contact must exist only in marriage between a man and a woman. Sexual intimacy outside of marriage is exploding through extramarital affairs, pornography, and premarital sex. These devalue and lower the sexual moral standard of God; hence, humanity refuses to acknowledge adultery as sin.

It's important to note that the church is both invisible, "the body of true believers" and visible." It consists of a local congregation. Many churches today are tolerant of or silent about sexual immorality within the church. Their leaders fail to challenge immoral dating habits among youth and their members. Rather they are becoming more like the society in which they live by permitting sin in the church because of modern times. In the book of Revelation, we see God condemning the church of Ephesus for engaging in and teaching that sexual immorality was covered in the Christian's faith and did not affect one's salvation; the church of Pegamos for teaching the doctrine of Balaam and compromising the believer's faith with immorality, worldliness, and false ideologies; and lastly the church of Thyatira for allowing "Jezebel" to seduce the people to commit fornication. God's response to those three churches was for them to repent. The church is the bride of Christ, and He will not be tolerant of sexual immorality within the church (Revelation 2:6, 14, 20).

Churches that are tolerant of sexual perverseness are not adhering to the standards of God and are desecrating the body of Christ. By accepting such behavior, the people of God are becoming more like society and the world. Pastors and leaders in the church who permit such acts open the door for sexual impurity and shameful lust to enter their lives. They seek only for self-gratification and to receive worldly accolades for themselves rather than to bring glory to God. Churches should not be tolerant of sexual immorality; instead, they should denounce such pagan acts, discipline the church, and mourn over the defilement and degradation of God's people and His Word.

The following are three reasons for disciplining the church:

- Publicly bringing honor to God
- Publicly displaying God's standard of holiness
- Publicly displaying purity of the church

God is holy, and those who worship Him should worship Him in spirit and in truth. The church is the physical representative of Christ; therefore, it should be holy as He is holy, united by the Holy Spirit and diligently seeking faithful relationship with God. The church is where the spirit, presence, and power of Christ are manifested; hence, God gives us leaders in the church to equip the saints to do His will and to be loyal to the gospel and its teachings. They must stand in humility, exhibit fear before the presence of God, be vitally concerned for the purity of the church, and be loyal to biblical faith. They must discipline members who commit such sins, thereby preserving godly character and righteous standards.

Sexual immorality is destructive and harmful. It creates a romantic and fluffy feeling that comes with consequences in our physical bodies, such as sexually transmitted disease and God's rejection. From the scripture, there are many stories of God's abandonment of humanity because of sexual immorality, for example, the story of Sodom and Gomorrah and the flooding in Noah's time. They chose to reject the truth of God's Word and seek pleasure in unbiblical practices and ungodliness. A primary sign of God's abandonment of any society or people is that they start becoming obsessed with sexual immorality and perversion (Romans 1:24).

The following are three stages of God's abandonment:

- He gives them over to a depraved mind
- He gives them over to sexual pleasures that degrade the body
- He gives them over to unnatural passion

These three stages occur for those who reject the truth of God's revelation, seek pleasures in ungodliness, and believe in Satan's lies. As a result, the scripture tells us that God has already pronounced His judgement on them. The purpose of God's abandonment is to allow sin and its consequences to accelerate as part of His judgment upon humanity and to make them realize that there is an Almighty God and their need from Him in their lives.

The following sexual acts are an abomination to God:

- Cross-dressing (Deuteronomy 22:5)
- Homosexuality (Leviticus 18:22)
- Sexual rituals (Deuteronomy 23:18)

Any sexual sin that is a defilement of the gift of sexuality and also dishonors marriage is an abomination unto God. Sexual activities with a person of the same sex are unnatural. Sodomy is an abomination to the Lord God. Because of the gravity of this sexual act, it is condemned in the Holy Scriptures over five times. Looking at this world that we are living in today, we can see signs of God's wrath, which is being poured out on those who have become obsessed with sexual immorality and perversion and those who indulge in such acts. God intensifies their lust for this forbidden sexual act as He gives them up to uncleanliness.

Jesus Christ warns mankind through Lot's wife, who turned into a pillar of salt, that those whose hearts are attached to the world's present system will not be spared from His wrath and the destruction that is to come upon the ungodly. Lot's wife placed her affections on an earthly society rather than upon heaven. The question everyone should ask him- or herself about the lesson learned from Lot's wife is "What is my heart more attached to—earthly things or the hope of Christ's return?" Lot escaped the destruction of Sodom; however, he lost his family, and his descendants became pagan because of the sin of incest that took place between him and his daughters (Genesis 19: 26).

The world finds no pleasure in having real intimacy with God; rather, it's only in false ideology of self-satisfaction and pleasures of this world that offer pleasure for now but eternal pain forever. This world is certainly like Sodom and Gomorrah, a clear indication that it is currently in the hands of Satan for sin, idolatry, and sexual perversion take over and mankind falls prey to this world system. No longer do they regard marriage as between a man and a woman. Men want to be women and vice versa by changing their sexual organs. They believe that homosexuality is right. Basically, all that God says is wrong, now becomes right as the world stage continually displays the lust of the flesh, thereby making it increasingly more difficult for humanity to be obedient to God's command.

God has called us to moral and sexual purity. Thus, He requires His followers to live by the high standard of purity and sanctification, refraining from sexual acts and things that may incite emotional desires. This means restraint and avoidance of any activity that would defile one's purity before God. Therefore, we ought to control our bodies and not give in to the lust of the flesh or the eyes. That caution is for both the single and the married. God's temple, "your body," must be holy because He is holy, and He made His followers' bodies holy by the sanctifying work of the Holy Spirit and the power of the cross.

Purity is important to God because He is pure, and He desires us to be the same. Purity is not limited only to our sexuality. It should also include our thought life, words, and behaviors. Being sexually pure can only be accomplished through the help of the Holy Spirit of Christ, our obedience to God, and having self-control, which is one of the fruits of the spirit. Followers of Christ, although they live in an immoral world, should not compromise God's holiness, truth, or themselves by accepting such a lifestyle and lowering their holy standards in accommodating its values and trends.

Here is how to refrain from sexual immorality:

- Abstain from sex
- Exercise self-control
- Flee from lustful desires and evil
- Know that your body is the temple of God
- Sanctify your body unto God
- Seek the help of the Holy Spirit

God wants us to be morally pure; hence, he plainly states in His will "to abstain from sexual immorality." Instead, He wants mankind to increase their pleasure in Him, for His Word says, "at His right hand are pleasure forever"(Psalms

16:11). As followers of Christ, we must live holy and pure lives before Him, for it is the will of God. Jesus Himself said, "Blessed are the pure in heart for they shall see God." The pure in heart are those who have been delivered from sin's power. The heart, which includes our minds, wills, and emotions, must seek the things of God, having the same attitude of heart that God has, a love for righteousness, and a hatred of sin (Matthew 5:8).

God has not called us unto uncleanliness but to holiness, and when we follow His commands, we are honoring God with our bodies. We are wholeheartedly committed to God and separated from all that offends Him, being blameless in holiness. We ought to be holy in both body and spirit with a greater commitment to God and totally occupied with Him, His Word, obeying, and be of service to Him with our greatest attention toward our heavenly home. We are told in the scriptures, "the unrighteous shall not inherit the kingdom of God"(1Corintians 6:9). Therefore, anyone who does not have fellowship with Christ, has disowned Him, and lives in immorality will be declared spiritually dead and will not see God.

Followers of Christ must live sober, righteous, and godly lives in this world. The marking of God is upon our lives; hence, our bodies must never be defiled by any immorality or evil, whether immoral thoughts, desires, deeds, books, magazines, the internet, and so on. Moreover, do not approve of the immorality and perverseness of this world or engage in unbiblical actions. In doing such, you are subjecting yourself to the same judgment as those who participate in and entertain themselves with evil and immorality (2 Thessalonians 2:11–12).

Repent from Idolatry

The direct words of the Almighty God and the first two commandments of the Ten Commandments are "Thou shalt have no other gods before me; and thou shalt not make unto thee any graven image"(Exodus 20:3). These commands prohibit humanity from worshipping or calling upon any of the gods of this world.

Idolatry is a sin and is defined as believing in any person, institution, or thing as having equal or greater authority than God and His Word. Simply put, idolatry is allowing material things to become the focus of a person's desires and values instead of God. Idolatry is a pagan religion and the occult of magic, which includes violence, magical arts, drugs, witchcraft, and occult worship. It always involves the worshipping of demons. It is the activities of Satan to separate one from the true God. It starts with the acknowledgment of a power that controls natural forces that then indwells an object, such as stone and wood.

Idolatry starts in the heart of a person craving, wanting, enjoying, or being satisfied by something that he or she treasures the most in life. This often occurs whenever humans give themselves over to greed and materialism rather than trust in God alone. It's also participating in immorality and the wickedness of this world. Idolatry is the foremost sin of a covetous heart. It leads one to desire more than what God provides. Thus people put their trust in something or someone that is lesser than God for their needs. A covetous heart is never contented. They always seek more to feel secure and please the self, placing all their affection on themselves, their possessions, and earthly rather than heavenly things (Colossians 3:5).

Becoming involved in idolatry is a matter of the heart, pride, self-centeredness, and greed, which all leads to rebellion against God. It is important to know that idolatry extends beyond the worship of idols, images, and false gods. It comes out of a consciousness of need or recognition, for it begins when one rejects or refuses to know about Almighty God, the creator of heaven and the sustainer of life. The apostle Paul tells us to flee from idolatry because it expresses a foolish heart that is darkened and will only bring spiritual death, as mankind would not inherit the kingdom of God but instead would be reserved for hellfire (1 Corinthians 10:14).

Why does mankind fall into idolatry?

- They harden their hearts toward God
- They refuse to acknowledge the existence of God
- They refuse to give thanks to God
- They refuse to glorify God
- They reject the knowledge of God through creation

Falling into idolatry does not just happen. It is a progression. It is the demise of one's moral and spiritual nature, as he or she loses sight of his or her own identity and thus turns to idolatry. Deep down within, these people know that God does exist but choose to suppress that truth. Instead, they become futile in their own speculations as their hearts hardens toward God. Sin and hardheartedness produce restlessness and ungodly practices, and eventually their lives will spiral out of control. They begin living on the edge, as they are now controlled by Satan. Their main priority in life will be to seek more pleasure in the ways of the world. They believe that they can trust in their own understanding and that they control the course of their lives.

In the scripture, we have seen idolatry recurring throughout the history of God's people. The first record of such was in the family of Jacob, where God told him to put away the strange gods. Also, we see the first story recorded where the children of Israel engaged in idolatry as they built and worshipped the golden calf while Moses was on Mount Sinai. Again, during the period of the judges, the people of God frequently worshipped idols. King Solomon also set in motion the same constant pattern of idolatry in Israel. Idolatry was so attractive to the people of Israel because they were surrounded by pagan nations that believed in the worshipping of several gods. They felt that it was superior to worshipping one God. The Israelites were imitating the other nations rather than being obedient to God's command to "be holy and separate themselves"(Leviticus 20:26). Instead, they felt that they were justified in worshipping other gods (Exodus 32:2–4).

God's covenant with the people of Israel from the beginning was based on exclusive worship of Him alone. They were commanded to fear and serve only Him. For the New Testament believers, this same command applies. All our worship should be directed to Almighty God alone. We must be totally consecrated to God and His purpose in our life. We are to love the Lord God with our whole heart. We are warned in the scripture against idolatry and to flee from it. Jesus Himself tells us that "we cannot serve

God and mammon"; either we hate one or love the other (Deuteronomy 5:7; Matthew 6:24).

Idolatry is classified as follows:

- The worship of animals
- The worship of animated objects
- The worship of heroes or celebrities
- The worship of money
- The worship of the powers of nature

Throughout the scripture, idols were mostly created by hand, a carved image made of wood or stone. Idols can either be physical objects that represent or symbolize a deity or abstract concepts like greed. An idol is any image or representation of a god used as an object of worship. It's anything that replaces or place ahead of the one true God, such as a career, a relationship, a sport, possessions, an addiction, and so on. Idol worship is a transgression of God's law, and it is disobedience to God, as it breaks the first two commandments, which are especially against the worship of spirits through spiritism and all forms of idolatry. The prohibition against the worship of other gods required that no image be made of them; nor should anyone make an image of who they believe God is or what He looks like and worship it. He is too great to be represented by anything made with human hands.

Followers of Christ must direct their worship to God alone. No worshipping, praying, or seeking guidance or help from any other gods, spirits, or the dead. This kind of action represents spiritual unfaithfulness to the Lord God, and it is forbidden. We are called not to worship or create such images because it is impossible for any image to truly represent the glory and characteristics of God; hence, the scripture asks, "to whom will ye liken God, or will ye compare unto Him?" (Isaiah 40:18). Any image of Him dishonors God and detracts from His true nature and from what He reveals about Himself. God is a spirit. He is holy and unsearchable. Therefore, our concept of God must not be based on pictures or images of your belief of how He looks but rather on His Word and the revelation of His son, Jesus Christ.

Idols are mere pieces of wood or stone carved by human hands. They have no power of their own, as they are vain objects. Hence, the scripture makes it clear that idols in and of themselves are nothing; therefore, they cannot limit the power of God. Behind every idol are devils or evil spirits that are controlled by Satan. The power behind idolatry is the power and activities of demons. In today's world, idols have great power, as they are influenced and controlled by Satan. There is a relationship between idolatry and demons because pagan religions practice it. It is linked to sorcery, divination, enchantment, witchcraft, and so on. All these practices involve paying homage to demons and the devil. It's important to note that false gods and religions are the spiritual realities of devils and demons.

Idols are blocks of stone or wood, and their powers only exist in the mind, the natural corruption of the heart, and the displaying of arrogance of the worshippers, as this activity involves deception, various forms of bondage, and oppression. They worship these idols to seek solace from the hardship of life, because people feel that God is not answering their prayers, they can't wait on God, or they just don't believe in Him. What humanity needs to realize is that no idol can infuse our lives with meaning, worth, or eternal hope. Instead, an idolatrous pursuit will only leave people empty, unsatisfied, and ultimately destroyed. Such practice brings down the wrath of God, for the Holy Scripture tells us, "God is a jealous God"; our worship, praise, and honor should belong to God alone; and any type of idol worship will only provoke Him to anger (Exodus 34:14).

In today's world, like that of the Old Testament times, idolatry is a powerful tool that the devil uses to turn mankind away from God. The pleasures of life and material gains divert or consume them quickly and drive mankind's attention away from serving God. They are preoccupied with achieving earthly goals to satisfy their own desires. When earthly things become great to a person, it naturally diverts their minds and hearts from hearing the voice of God or recognizing Him as Lord, as their thoughts go on self—me, me—which can be one's greatest idol. Mankind has started becoming a self-involved generation.

The idolatry of oneself consists of the following:

- The lust of the flesh
- The lust of the eyes
- The lust of the pride of life

These are called the worshipping of self, the worship of materialism, which then builds up one's ego through the acquisition of more, better, and newer things. This is plainly called covetousness. The scripture also forbids coveting, as it is a sin. Furthermore, the apostle Paul states that covetousness is equated with immorality and impurity. Covetousness is at the root of different types of sin. Thus, Jesus gave a stern warning about it: "Beware of covetousness"(Luke 12:15). Covetousness never brings satisfaction and contentment because those who desire to be rich will fall into many temptations and hurtful desires that will only ruin their lives here on earth and throughout eternity

From the beginning of creation, in the garden of Eden, Satan tempted Eve to eat from the tree of life with these words: "You will be as gods"(Genesis 3:5). He is using that same tactic on mankind as they now call themselves God, believing that they do not need the Almighty God. Humanity, in seeking to be as gods, becomes independent from the Almighty God, as they determine their own standards for living and become false gods. Adam and Eve attempted to be as God's equal and sinned. Through their fall, humanity became, to some extent, independent of God; hence, God warned that all who seek to be gods shall perish from the earth and from under the heavens

Why is idolatry attractive?

- Mankind creates their own gods
- Mankind has a sense of power and control
- Mankind's heart is deceitful

Idolatry became attractive to mankind in both the Old and New Testament and in today's world because it is convenient, easy, and self-pleasing, and it does not require much discipline. It promotes self-worship. That is what fuels idolatry because mankind wants to be valued, praised, and even envied by others. Mankind finds these objects desirable, and they give themselves over to their pursuit and attractiveness and thus start becoming loyal. They develop a bond to their gods or idols. In the mind of the worshipper, these idols help them to obtain what they want. Moreover, they consider themselves to be strong, in control, and dominant. Because of this false worshipping, they become self-sufficient and self-reliant. However, idolatry on a whole does not bring lasting satisfaction, for it requires heavy sacrifice, and it reduces one's humanity. It leaves one feeling alone and empty as its demands become more insistent.

In some religions and societies today, people are praying to and worshipping images. They embrace a multitude of gods and goddesses, as they desire to have supernatural contact with the spirit world.

The sun, moon, stars, and things that God intended to serve as signs that point to Him, mankind also worships. People twist the intended purpose of them by creating a false theory that the stars and the planets guide the lives of people. These religions worship statues and exalt other people, images, and objects above God. They also communicate with the dead. That is essentially communication with demons, which is forbidden in the scripture (Deuteronomy 18:10–12).

Satan is a master deceiver, and he uses idolatry and false religion to turn mankind's hearts away from God. These religions are deeply rooted in the desires of the flesh, which include pride and self-love, and their approach is to encourage a self-focused person. He desires to be worshipped; therefore, he uses his demons and false doctrines to deceive mankind to pledge allegiance to evil spirits, having mankind usurp God's rightful place in their hearts and turn it over to Satan. Satan is the god of this world, and he exercises great power in this evil world, where he can create counterfeit miracles, signs, and wonders. Undoubtedly, his powers sometimes contribute to the prosperity of the wicked, as he and his demons can give material benefits to those who worship him and are living by his principles and desires.

Idolatry is a dangerous offense to God, for it diminishes the glory of God. In worshipping any image or idol, people are exchanging the glory of the incorruptible God for an idol in the form of a corruptible man, animal, and so on. The danger of participation in idolatry is facing the wrath of God; hence, He frequently warned against such in the Old Testament and judged the children of Israel. They were taken into captivity by Babylon. God tells us in the scripture, "I will not give my glory to another," which means that He is possessive of the worship and service that belong to Him (Jeremiah 32:36).

The elders of Israel were guilty of idolatry in their hearts, as they were not loyal to God and His word. They desired the ungodly way of life, and for this forbidden act, God refused to guide them and answer their prayers. In similar manner, those today who have idols in their hearts and seek guidance from God will find no help from Him because their hearts are filled with ungodly desires and the sinful things of this world. Having idols in one's heart causes a stumbling block and a stronghold in a person's life. There's good news, however. God is a faithful and loving God, and for those who are guilty of having idols in their hearts and want them removed, He is willing to help. First, they must sincerely turn to Him by repenting of their sins and then completely commit themselves over to God in faith and obedience. Then He will be their God and extinguish all ungodliness within them (Ezekiel 6).

How do you remove idols from your heart?

- Believe in Almighty God
- Center your affections on Jesus Christ
- Place your affections on things above
- Read and study the Word of God
- Repent of your sins
- Trust in the power of God

For those who turn back to God through repentance and resist the tendency toward idolatry and other sinful practices, God promised He would help, care for, guide, and protect them if they consistently maintain their walk with Him. In newness of life in Christ, they must recognize that they are up against spiritual forces of evil. They must fervently be committed to God's truth and righteousness and know that Satan's stronghold on their lives has been broken by God. They must proclaim the gospel of the kingdom of God, confess of the power of the cross and the effectiveness of Jesus's blood, and be a testimony of the greatness of God's power in their lives.

How does one avoid falling into idolatry?

- Acknowledge God as sovereign
- Give your life to God Almighty
- Guard your heart from sinful desires
- Obey God's commands
- Study God's Word

- Trust only in God
- Wait on God's timing
- Worship God daily

In loving God with all our heart, mind, and body, there will not be any room for idolatry when we realize that He is the creator of all things, and He alone has the wisdom and power to determine what is good and evil. God declared in His Word through the prophets that He is the only true God, and all others are merely images of false gods, for He alone can bring salvation and everlasting life and give peace that passes all understanding. God alone is all knowing. God must be the sole source and standard for all human moral or spiritual conduct as defined in His Word, He requires His people to be obedient and maintain a faithful relationship with Him.

True followers of Christ must have as their purpose in life to seek, love, and worship God, relying solely on Him to provide that which is good and perfect in their lives. We have died to sin in God's sight and have been given the powers to resist sin and the evils of the world; therefore, we must never conform to the surrounding society and accept its way of life. Moreover, we continue to remain separated from the corrupt world system and from unholy compromise and draw near to God through our fellowship in prayers, worship, and persevering in the faith.

TWO

The Call to Salvation

SALVATION ORIGINATES FROM GOD; IT is from Him that all grace flows. It is the act of being delivered, redeemed, or rescued, as it deals with the eternal, spiritual deliverance from the consequences of sin. Salvation is a gift from God that is based on His unmerited favor toward humanity, provided through His Son's sacrificial death on the cross and His resurrection. The scripture tells us that "when we were enemies with God, He reconciled us to Himself by the death of His Son" (Romans 5:10). Salvation cannot be earned; it is only available in Jesus Christ alone, and it is free to all mankind. Salvation begins in the head and not the heart, as it involves having a change of mind (John 14:6).

Salvation is a transaction with God based on His grace, received by faith and guaranteed by God. It's Him intervening in our lives because of His great love for us and the richness of His grace by which we can be saved. We are not only saved from something; we are saved also from someone and the bondage of sin. It is received by us through our response of faith in Christ Jesus. God planned salvation, and Jesus and the Holy Spirit prepared the way of salvation. The scripture tells us that "sin separates us from God"(Isaiah 59:2). Therefore, without the divine intervention of God, all humans were destined to eternal separation and into hellfire. Hence, we need salvation to save us from the penalty of sin.

The means of salvation come directly from the gospel of Christ, "the Good News," which is the power of God unto salvation when we hear, receive, and believe the truth of His Word. According to the scriptures, there is no salvation in any other than Jesus Christ. This truth reveals the exclusive nature of the gospel and the responsibility of those of us preaching and teaching the gospel to all mankind. Moreover, it is the guarantee of life in the future and in this present life, as it is opposed to death, which is eternal life without God. Salvation is a matter of life and death, both literally and figuratively, because the quality of life now and in the future are at stake. It has both the present and future aspects of life. Present salvation is that which we receive from God in the gift of His grace, and the future salvation is our complete deliverance from sin when we will receive our immortal bodies and reign with Him in heaven (Acts 4:10–12).

What does salvation bring?

- The call to repentance
- The gift of grace

- The indwelling of the Holy Spirit
- The new birth or being born again

Salvation is interconnected to Christ's atonement, the human condition, and God's attributes, such as His justice and holiness. In receiving salvation, it's important to know who Jesus is, who He claimed to be, and what it means to believe, trust, and follow Him because salvation entails repentance and a sincere willingness to change our mind, heart, and behavior. Those are the central degrees of humility that are required from us to submit to Christ and receive the gift of salvation, as God is bringing us out of sin and into fellowship with Him through Jesus Christ. Moses told the people of Israel that God brought them "out" of Egypt so that He might bring them "into" the land of their fathers. That was the work of salvation for the people of Israel; it was a deliverance and a setting up of the people of Israel in the Promise Land (Deuteronomy 6:23).

Salvation does not come by mere efforts to keep the law. To those who were under the old covenant, salvation and a right relationship with God came through faith expressed by obedience to His law, for it was a sacrificial system. Those living by the law in Old Testament times displayed a measure of grace to God, as in those faithful believers such as Abraham, Noah, Enoch, and so on. No longer do we look to the Old Testament law and sacrifice for salvation and acceptance by God, for we have been separated from that covenant law and united with Christ. Rather it's by the Holy Spirit of Christ, His grace coming into our lives to regenerate our hearts and creating us into the image of Christ. Our salvation is procured by the payment of a

37

ransom. Jesus Christ paid this price to free mankind from bondage. He secured the ransom by shedding His blood and giving His life, and as a result, we are now free from the Old Testament law, sin's slavery, and Satan's dominion. This freedom in Christ results in righteousness and obedience to Jesus Christ. God's grace is fully available to all who believe.

From the story of the apostle Paul and Silas in prison, when the Philippian jailer asked Paul, "What can I do to be saved?" Paul responded, "Believe on the Lord Jesus." That same promise goes out to all those who want to receive God's gift of salvation. To believe in Jesus Christ is to focus our faith on Him, confess our sins, trust, and be obedient to Christ, knowing that He is our redeemer from sin, the only begotten Son of God. All this includes the working of God, who draws sinners to Himself, and the work of the Holy Spirit in convicting us of sins. Basically, it's saving faith and commitment to Jesus as our savior.

Repentance and faith all are included in the process of receiving salvation, as it's the result of God drawing our hearts toward Him, thus opening our eyes to the knowledge of His love and grace. Accordingly, the Old Testament and the New Testament both support the fact that faith in God has always been the avenue of salvation. The Old Testament saints were saved based on their response to the knowledge they had of God, their faith, looking forward to something they could not see. Faith has two designations, "trust in or reliance upon." This means to persevere in trust and belief by manifesting an obedience of faithfulness to God. This was the faith the Old Testament saints exhibited. A perfect example is Abraham, whom God counted as righteous. The Bible tells us, "By grace are we saved through faith; it is the gift of God." Importantly, know that both faith and grace are free gifts from God, as He bestows saving faith and saving grace, redeeming mankind from sin.

The benefits of salvation include the following:

- We are adopted into God's family
- We are justified by God
- We are reconciled to God
- We are saved from the power of sin
- We have access to God
- We receive the gift of grace

Receiving these benefits means that we were rescued from sin's bondage and brought into freedom; it also saved us from the wrath of God and brought us into peace with God, which are a result of the gift of God's grace. This gift is God placing in our heart a desire to know and serve Him, because without grace, salvation would be impossible. Grace and faith come from God. Therefore, to receive faith, first one must receive God's grace. For it's by grace we receive faith that enables us to believe that God has sent His Son. Saving grace comes through a person's faith in God, and faith is something that God produces in us through the workings of the Holy Spirit.

The grace of God is His love in action; it is expressed by God's forgiveness of sins and His blessings toward us now and in the future. Before grace, we were guilty of breaking God's law. We were enemies of God who were deserving of death. We were unrighteous, dead to Him, and destined for eternal punishment. However, God extended His grace and gave us victory over sin through Jesus Christ, who embodied grace and truth. The saving grace of God has appeared to everybody here on earth; it instructs mankind to reject sin, ungodliness, evil, and the pleasures of the world. However, it's important to know that God does not force a person to accept His grace. Rather, He gives us all the free will to choose. Grace is the means to believe through faith. Our faith then acts through our obedience in Christ. Those who accept His gift of grace and obey His commands He then empowers to live righteous and godly lives while awaiting the return of Jesus Christ (Titus 2:11).

The first manifestation of God's grace was in the garden of Eden when God killed an animal to cover Adam and Eve, and from that point onward, God was determined to conquer Satan by reconciling humanity to Himself at the cost of the life of His Son. In the Old Testament, God revealed Himself as the God of grace who showed love to His people and His desire to be faithful to the covenant promise He made to Abraham, Isaac, and Jacob. In the New Testament, God showed His grace by the giving of His Son for the undeserving sinners who are under condemnation. His grace is giving us what we do not deserve: His goodness, favor, kindness, and mercy. The only way we can enter a relationship with God is by Him choosing to make a way so mankind can be in right standing with Him (Genesis 3:21, Ephesians 2:4–5).

God's grace and power are seen clearly and profoundly in humans' weakness. The greater the weakness, the more grace because the work of grace is not compulsory or irresistible. Instead, it is always dependent on our cooperation and response to faith. God's grace motivates obedience to Him, which leads to righteousness. His grace establishes a moral ground and an obligation to holiness as we are now dead to sin; therefore, we can now accomplish the will of God. His grace is an energizing strength that flows from the risen Christ and operates through the Holy Spirit indwelling the lives of His followers to serve others and to demonstrate our spiritual gifts to build up, encourage, and edify the body of Christ. Importantly, it's knowing that God's grace does not end when we become a follower of Christ; instead it continues throughout our lives as we live in Him. It works upon and within our lives.

In accepting God's grace, we receive the following:

- Abundant blessing
- Eternal treasures
- God's forgiveness
- Heaven as our final home
- His Holy Spirit
- Reconciliation with God

A follower of Christ's life from the beginning to the end is dependent on the grace of God, as it is to will and to do His good pleasure, to grow in Christ and to witness for Him. Grace assures us of God's forgiveness and guarantees His discipline when we disobey Him. It erases the eternal consequences of our sins but does not exempt us from the temporal consequences of our sins that we commit daily, thus the importance of repenting daily. This grace of God is beneficial to us, as it provides forgiveness from sin. It gives us gifts for the present, such as His wisdom, knowledge, and goodness, for it imparts acceptance and power to do His will, thereby giving us hope for the future. We must diligently desire and seek after God's grace, humbling ourselves before God, studying and obeying His Word, praying without ceasing, and continually being filled with the Holy Spirit of Christ.

One important aspect of God's grace we ought to be mindful of is that it can be resisted and abandoned by people, as they believe in God but do not believe the process through which salvation came. They become resistant to God's grace by harboring bitterness and resentment toward God's discipline, the church, and others, abandoning faith and the teaching of the gospel of Christ. Resistance to God's grace also happens when followers only observe the law, which cannot impart life, because it's only through faith in Christ and the supernatural manifestation of the Holy Spirit in our lives that mankind can obtain eternal life.

Faith is another important aspect of salvation, as it is God's *sole* requirement for receiving the gift of grace. It is through having faith only in Jesus Christ that God provides forgiveness of sins and eternal life to all who receive His grace. Faith means firmly believing and trusting in the crucified and risen Christ as our savior, which involves believing with our whole heart, yielding up our wills and committing ourselves to Him. This includes repentance, obedience to God and His Word, and having a heartfelt personal devotion to Him that expresses itself in trust, love, gratitude, and loyalty to Him. It brings us into a new relationship with God and exempts us from His wrath. Without faith, it is impossible to please God. This means that we must believe in Him even though we cannot see Him, for this is a key part of receiving salvation, and when mankind exhibits faith in God, He in turn blesses us. Faith is actualized by our will to trust in Jesus Christ.

According to the scripture, "faith is the assurance of things hoped for, the evidence of things not seen"(Hebrews 11:1). This is demonstrating faith and trusting in God in all situations, which enables a person to persevere and be loyal to Him. Faith is believing in the true and living God without seeing Him. Faith is a gift from God, which is accompanied with His grace and mercy. It is not something that we can work for or conjure up on our own. It comes only by belief in the risen Christ. We are not saved *by* faith but *through* faith. Our faith is only reliable by the object of our faith, which is Jesus Christ. Subsequently, only then do we realize that no one can work for their salvation. Rather, our faith is what connects our needs with God's provision to provide salvation (Ephesians 2:8–9).

Our faith in God must be genuine and not just a belief. Demons also do believe in God; therefore, true faith must accept the deity of Jesus Christ as the only begotten Son of God, His death, and His resurrection. Faith is trusting in the risen Christ, which is the marking of genuine faith. Demonstrating such faith shows our love and belief in God as we live by faith and receive God's glorious joy as a gift. Through faith, we obtain knowledge about God through our five senses and our intellect. We understand things in the spiritual realm, that happens at the spirit level through revelation. The natural mind cannot understand things given by God, which includes creation, for it's only a renewed mind in Christ that can comprehend such things (James 2:19).

Here are some elements of faith:

- It believes in God's goodness
- It has confidence in God's Word
- It leads to righteousness
- It obeys God's commands
- It seeks God

Faith believes in spiritual realities and regulates life on the promises of God. It rejects the pleasures of sin and the evils of this world and perseveres in testing, endures persecution, performs acts of righteousness, and does not return to the sinful world. Faith in Jesus Christ is the act of a single moment and a continuing attitude that must be nurtured and strengthened, so our faith becomes greater and that we may not stagger at the promises of God through unbelief. Followers of Christ ought to have the faith of Abraham, for his faith endured, believed, trusted, obeyed, grew strong, and gave glory to God. That kind of faith marks us as true followers of Christ, saved by believing in the promises of God.

Saving faith is trusting in the gospel of Christ and believing it to be true, as it involves the work of the Spirit of Christ as well as a person's willingness to believe. An unbeliever is dead spiritually and requires God to draw him or her to Christ, which is the conviction of sin, His righteousness, and His judgment. To receive saving faith, a person must know about Jesus Christ. Genuine faith believes in God and leads to confession of sins and obedience to Christ, thus producing good work after salvation, Hence, the scripture tells us that faith and work do not bring salvation; rather faith produces good work after salvation. Mankind is *not* justified by works but by faith in God, who imparts righteousness to the ungodly who believe in Him. Moreover, saving faith is rooted in God's grace, His promises, and reliance on God's power.

Here are three elements of saving faith:

- A commitment to fully trusting and relying on God
- A willingness to follow God
- A knowledge and understanding of God

There are two biblical truths to faith: a person is saved through faith; however, faith that saves is not alone because faith that hath not works is dead, according to the scripture. Saving faith involves both the mind and our will. Saving faith is a living faith in a living savior that not only confesses Jesus as savior but also obeys Him. Obedience is an essential aspect of true faith. It must be an active and enduring faith that shapes our very existence, showing sincere devotion to God and His Word. True saving faith expresses itself in godly actions and works by love, for it cannot avoid expressing itself in love motivated by works. Works without faith are dead works, and faith without works is dead faith. True faith always manifests itself in obedience to God, and compassionate and righteous work done for others in need. Subsequently, mankind cannot maintain a living faith by trusting in their own works; rather it's the grace of God, the power and work of Jesus Christ, and the indwelling of the Holy Spirit that enable us to respond to God by faith and be receptive to Him.

Followers of Christ must always remember that salvation

is based solely on what God has done for us and not what we can do for Him. The proper response to salvation is to be in constant prayer to God, which will keep our hearts, work, and lives free to continually please Him. One of the greatest things about salvation is that we, the followers of Christ, look only to Jesus Christ, who is our high priest, our mediator who opens the way for us to come to God the Father with confidence for all area of need in life. God sympathizes with our weaknesses; therefore, we can confidently approach His throne of grace, knowing that our prayers are received and desired by Him because His grace flows with His love, help, mercy, and spiritual gifts—all that we need in any circumstances.

Here are four principles about salvation:

- Salvation is important as it manifests God's love and glory
- Salvation is important for edification of the saints
- Salvation is important in evangelizing sinners
- Salvation is important to the souls of mankind

The basis of salvation is God's grace. The means of salvation is Christ's death. The channel of our salvation is our faith. The result of salvation is good works, and the confidence of salvation is that what God started, He will finish. The salvation of all humanity depends upon the faithful proclamation of the solemn truths of God's Word by which the spirit produces conviction in the sinner.

Be Justified

Justification or to be justified means to be acquitted, declared "not guilty." It is where a person is declared to be righteous or be in right standing in the sight of God, which comes out of our belief by faith in Jesus Christ. It brings the peace of God into the lives of His followers, as we are assured of our salvation. Justification enables God to begin the process of sanctification, which is decisive for eternity, as it brings new life and eternal life for all who believe. This marks the beginning of an abundant life in Christ. Justification lets sinners know that their sins are forgiven, and they are free from all guilt. Justification does not come by merely obeying the law. Instead, it signifies conformity to the law of God after one accepts Christ. Basically, justification comes by God's grace, mercy, love, and forgiveness (Romans 3:28, Titus 3:7).

Justification by faith upholds the law according to its right purpose and function. Through reconciliation with God and the regeneration work of the Holy Spirit, followers of Christ honor and obey God's moral law. It's important to know that the law is insufficient to redeem us apart from God's grace. It is powerless to deliver us from our sinful nature and sinful desires, because in only obeying the law, a person will struggle on his or her own against the powers of sin. Moreover, he or she would not be able to attain justification. Therefore, in attempting to live life free from the bondage of sin, all efforts will be useless if we are not truly born again, reconciled to God, and redeemed from Satan's power. Rather it is the Holy Spirit working in our lives, allowing us to live lives of righteousness, which is seen as the fulfilment of God's moral law, hence the operation of grace and obedience to the law of God (Romans 7:4–15).

God justifies sinners solely based on the work of Christ, for He was delivered unto death and was raised to life for our justification, which completely dealt with the guilt of mankind's sins. The justification of life for all mankind is potential, because it is actualized in individuals as they believe in Christ and receive His grace, life, and the gift of righteousness. God's righteousness is imputed onto us, declaring us righteous. Justification changes mankind's status before God, for when He looks at the shed blood of Jesus Christ, His death, He regards it to be the perfect sacrifice that covers all sins. Furthermore, whenever God looks at us, He only sees the atoning blood of His Son.

The importance of justification is as follows:

- We become a new creation
- We become heirs of God's kingdom
- We are found not guilty
- We are free from condemnation

Justification involves both the redemptive grace of Jesus Christ and the work of the Holy Spirit, resulting in humanity's relationship with God. Justification is based entirely on our obedience to Christ, His righteousness, and faith in Him. Our justification allows us to stand before the presence of God without guilt or condemnation because His grace provides freedom to break away from the bondage of sin and enter new life with Christ. Justification by faith declares a person righteous before God. Righteousness is a product of God's grace, which is given to mankind because of their trust and belief in Jesus Christ.

We are justified freely by God's grace through faith and the redemption of Christ. This process is vital, as it separates true biblical holiness from all the other religious belief systems, for in other religions, people must work their way to God. However, in true biblical standards, people have access to God by His grace through faith in Christ Jesus. The scripture tells us that "all have sinned and fall short of the glory of God" (Romans 3:23). This means we are all sinful in nature and guilty before God, hence the need for humanity being made righteous through the process of justification or being justified by God. Apart from having been redeemed, no one has kept his or her heart clean and pure from the guilt of sin. Moreover, it's only those who have come to God for forgiveness and cleansing who have a pure heart. Only by God's grace and redemption can anyone live a life with a conscience void of offense toward God and man

The following are important truths about justification:

- It is a gift from God
- It is grounded in the finished work of Christ
- It is the first of the conversion experience
- It is related to our forgiveness

Justification is the judicial aspect of the conversion experience, wherein the believer is viewed from God's perspective. He sees us wrapped in perfect righteousness; this righteousness is not our own but Christ's. It is that aspect of conversion that features our standing before a holy God. There are many blessings that take place after a believer's conversion, such as regeneration or being born again and the indwelling of the Holy Spirit. We are given as a witness of the spirit that we belong to the family of God. It's through the finished work of Christ that anyone can be justified by the redemption of Christ because sinners are declared guilty by the law and condemned to eternal death.

One might ask what it means to be righteous. It is acting in according with the divine or moral law of God. It is a behavior that is justifiable and right toward people and God. It is impossible for a person to be righteous on his or her own merit because such a standard is too high; however, it's only through the forgiveness of sins and the indwelling of the Holy Spirit that such can be attained. There is none righteous apart from Jesus Christ. People become righteous when they are in right relationship with God, thus receiving His salvation. The scripture tells us that the righteous can expect God to deliver and help them in times of trouble; they can appeal to God based on a clear conscience and a sincere endeavor to maintain the uprightness of their hearts as they assert spiritual integrity before God (Psalm 34:17).

The scripture says, "Many are the afflictions of the righteous" (Psalm 34:19), meaning believing in God and living righteously will *not* keep us from suffering in this life. Commitment to God often brings testing and persecution. Those who uphold God's standards of truth, justice, and purity will face rejection, criticism, persecution, and opposition. However, we, as followers of Christ, ought to rejoice because suffering for God imparts the highest blessings. We must be mindful of temptation that compromises God's will and refuse to compromise with the evil of this present world or its lifestyles. Loyalty to Christ, His truth, and His righteous standards involves constant determination not to compromise our faith or biblical standards. According to God's Word, those who suffer and endure persecution because of righteousness are promised rewards and the kingdom of heaven

How does one have victory over suffering?

- Believe that God cares for you
- Believe that God will bring you through
- Earnestly pray and seek God's help
- Know your suffering for Christ
- Read God's Word for strength
- Seek discernment from God

Regardless of how severe the circumstance, know that God is with us, for He promised that "He will never leave us nor forsake us" (Hebrews 13:5). He will be our help; therefore, we must be of a good courage, persevering in tribulation, trusting in God, and fully obeying Him even in our trying times. During the time of tribulation, we must always put on the full armor of Christ and cast our problems on God's grace, strength, and comfort. We must be acting with wisdom in accordance with God's Word, thereby avoiding anything that will remove us from God's protective care.

Jesus Christ, while on earth, was perfect even in tribulation, for He demonstrated the righteousness of God. Hence, His Word states that our righteousness is also Christ Himself, living within our hearts, and through Him, we become in Him the righteousness of God. We are a new creation in character and moral state, which is founded upon and flows from our faith in Christ, being controlled by the love of Christ and being representatives of God, His righteousness in this world. The righteousness of God is manifested and experienced by us when we remain in Christ, keep His Word in our hearts, obey His commands, and live in union and fellowship with Christ while in this evil world.

The righteousness of God is very prominent in relation to salvation. God not only justifies sinners, but He is also shown to be just or righteous in the process, as He upholds the moral order of the universe and is righteous without sin. His righteousness refers to His redemptive activity in the sphere of mankind's sins, for He is just and puts us in a right standing with Him because of His love for righteousness, which liberates us from the powers of evil. God's righteousness is an expression of His holiness and purity, which is opposed to sin; thus, He reveals His wrath against every form of wickedness, unbelief, and unjust treatment of others. For God to satisfy His justice, He sent Jesus Christ into the world as His gift of love, His sacrifice for sin, to reconcile humanity unto Himself. In the New Testament, Jesus Christ is called "the just one." God revealed Himself in Jesus Christ because in Him all the fullness of the deity of God lives (Colossians 2:9).

Jesus spoke of the righteousness of the scribes and Pharisees. Their righteousness was external only. They kept many rules, prayed, praised God, and read God's Word; however, they substituted their outward acts for the inward attitudes that come with a being born again person. These types of people only honor God with their mouths while their hearts are far away from God. They also appear righteous outwardly, but inwardly, they have no love for God. Followers of Christ, in upholding the righteousness of God, must always take refuge in Christ and remain committed to righteousness even if the moral and spiritual foundations are destroyed by society. The church must love righteousness by exercising caution. The righteousness that God requires of His followers is that their hearts and spirits are not only their outward deeds. Instead, they must conform to God's will in obedience, faith, and love.

True righteousness is "not" based upon external appearance but on God-based righteousness, upon the assessment of the heart. The prophet Habakkuk emphasized that only those who are justified by faith possess actual inward righteousness. Justification involves an inner righteousness through the indwelling of the Holy Spirit. Followers of Christ are obligated to remain justified because justification is accountability to God, for when He justifies us, He pardons us from past sins, thus the importance of living holy lives in the presence of God.

The benefits of justification include the following:

- Assurance of God's blessing
- God's grace
- Hope in God
- Peace with God
- Perseverance
- Reconciliation to God
- Salvation of God
- The Holy Spirit

Another important fact concerning justification is the new birth, "regeneration," which means the recreating of a new life or spiritual life in the human's heart by God and the Holy Spirit. Without the new birth, no one can see the kingdom of God or receive eternal life and salvation through Jesus Christ. Prior to accepting Christ, humans are, in their inherent nature and spirit, dead. All followers of Christ, because of their spiritual birth and faith in Jesus Christ, have the Holy Spirit, who is "the spirit of life," living within and constantly imparting His life to them as they surrender their lives to Him. Therefore, in this process of regeneration, God bestows to the believer's heart His nature, eternal life, and new creation in Christ Jesus, where he or she no longer conforms to the world but is a partaker of the divine nature of God, conformed to God and His holiness (Ephesians 4:24).

Becoming a new creation indicates that we belong to God totally, as His spirit rules our lives. We are now renewed after the image of Christ, sharing in His glory with a renewed knowledge and understanding. The life of the spirit is the regulating and activating power that frees us from the power of sin as we commit ourselves to obeying the spirit and pleasing God, living righteous lives, loving others, and avoiding a life of sin. Consequently, the new birth cannot be equated to the physical birth because the new birth is a matter of the spirit rather than the flesh. The spiritual or new birth comes when a person accepts Christ, a voluntary relationship that God desires from us and remains conditional based on our faith in Christ throughout our lives here on earth. The physical birth ties a father, mother, and child together in a bond or relationship that cannot be annulled.

In having the proper understanding of what it means to be justified by faith, people can receive the gift of God's grace as they begin to think that they are deserving of His salvation.

They are recipients of His grace, and justification is always free and completely an unmerited gift from God. The knowledge of justification and grace motivates good works and spiritual growth as we experience greater intimacy and oneness with God. We are compassionate to those whose lives are being destroyed by sin, identifying with God's attitude to righteousness and hatred of evil. Jesus's righteousness was justification that brings life for all those who believe. By His obedience, many will be made righteous because of justification, and the peace of God will rule in the hearts of mankind. Justification in our lives brings peace, joy, and contentment.

Be Sanctified

Biblical sanctification or being sanctified is the process of making holy, consecrating, separating from the world, and being set apart from sin unto God. The scripture tells us "to sanctity ourselves and be holy," (Leviticus 20: 7-8), which is the continual process of being made holy and in the image of Christ so we may have intimate fellowship with God and serve Him in sincere honesty of heart. Sanctification occurs because of salvation when the Holy Spirit enters our lives. However, this process does not stop at salvation, as it continues throughout our entire lives. We are sanctified for the purpose of worshipping and serving God. Jesus Christ is called "the holy one of God." He was made holy at conception. God the Father sanctified Him; hence, He is the sanctifier and model of sanctification, as we are made holy through the sacrifice of His life

The concept of sanctification is separation from the world, which is fundamental to God's relationship with

His people. This separation involves two dimensions: separating us morally and spiritually from sin and drawing us near to God in fellowship through prayer and worship. Sanctification is a requirement for all followers of Christ, as His desire is to sanctity our spirit, soul, and body, for without holiness, no man shall see God. The purpose of sanctification is to preserve holiness and righteousness so that we can be in a state of godliness, acceptable and pleasing to God because it is impossible to achieve sanctification through human effort. The good news about sanctification is that God has already accomplished it through the work of Jesus Christ, and it is appropriated through the Holy Spirit indwelling and leading in the lives of His people (Hebrews 12:14).Jesus Christ, while on earth, sanctified Himself by setting Himself apart to do the will of God. He suffered on the cross so His followers might be separated from the world and set apart for God to share in His glory. Jesus Christ is the one who sanctifies. The sanctified are those who are redeemed from the power of sin. It was God's goal to bring humans unto His glory by transforming them in His image. Jesus demonstrated the significance of sanctification as He prayed for His disciples before His crucifixion, for them to be set apart, to be near God, to live for Him and be like Him. The disciples' sanctification was accomplished by their devotion to the truth revealed to them by the Holy Spirit of truth, obedience to the Word, and the revelation of God's Holy Word (John 17:19).

The following are the requirements for sanctification:

• Being devotion to prayer

- Being filled with the Holy Spirit
- Being in intimate communion with Christ
- Being loving to righteousness and hating evil
- Being obedience to God
- Being sensitive to God's presence

To be sanctified, followers of Christ in our new nature must be in accordance with Christ, having an ethical righteousness of unblemished character that is demonstrated in purity, obedience, and blamelessness; we must be loving the Lord God with all our hearts, desiring His presence and fellowship, of a good conscience, dead to sin, and servants of righteousness unto holiness. We must put to death our sinful nature by renouncing it and embracing the power of the cross and the Holy Spirit daily as our source of victory. The apostle Peter charged us to sanctify Christ in our heart, having an inner reverence for and commitment to Christ, and always be ready to explain our faith in Christ to others in our witnessing (1 Peter 3:15).

Sanctification was God's will for the Israelites, as they were to live holy lives, separated from the lifestyle of the nations around them when God made that covenant with them at Mount Sinai. This covenant defined the conditions by which Israel would remain God's treasured possession. God intended for Israel to be a unique people, chosen, set apart to Him for His purpose, if they obeyed His commands. Through Israel, God wanted the other nations to see the wisdom and benefit of following His ways, but Israel was rebellious and unfaithful, for they did not obey God's commandments, which inflicted God's wrath upon them. Considering Israel's disobedience, the prophet Jeremiah prophesied that God would make a new covenant, which was accomplished by Jesus Christ "the Messiah" through His death and resurrection and the outpouring of the Holy Spirit upon His followers.

As New Testament followers of Christ, God also wants us to be His special people, holy, pure, and spiritually separated from the world. He gives us His holy aspiration to be like Him, producing in us His desires and His will to become sanctified and grow our relationship with Him with a change of attitude and behavior and conformity to His desires for our lives. Living holy lives through sanctification shows our dedication to and dependence on God's ability to work through us, as it requires discipline and a person's willingness to pursue it after sanctification wholeheartedly. This becomes more relevant to us as it is personal and deep. For it is all about obedience and accomplishing God's work within our lives as He fills us with His goodness and knowledge, thereby making us the light in this dark world.

What do we need to be spiritually separated from?

- Churches that commit sin and refuse to repent
- Cults
- False preachers, teachers,
- False religion
- Sin and evil
- The corrupt world system
- Ungodly compromise

Without a life of separation unto holiness, no one can claim the promises of God of being His sons and daughters. Followers of Christ's attitude must be one of hatred toward sin and opposition to false doctrine, this world system, and anything that is in direct opposition to God's very nature because He wants His people to be holy. This separation is a personal endeavor of all followers of Christ, to walk and live in a sanctified, separated manner, which is worthy of our calling in Jesus Christ, for it is vital in both the present and the future life. The purpose of spiritual separation is that followers of Christ might persevere in faith, purity, and love of God and testify about the truth and blessings of God's Word. Refusal to be spiritually separated will result in the loss of fellowship with Christ, acceptance by God, and our rights as His children (2 Corinthians 6:16–18, 7:1).

Sanctification involves a holy encounter with God and the awareness of His presence. As a living sacrifice unto Him, we continue to receive His grace and power to live holy lives. Experiencing Christ's nearness, love, and righteousness through prayer and the Holy Spirit results in us being transformed into His likeness. We should be participating in the Holy Spirit's sanctifying work, ceasing from sin and evil, purifying ourselves from all filthiness of the flesh, and not being polluted by the trends of this world. The process of being sanctified takes the work of the Holy Spirit and our willingness to accomplish God's will of sanctification, as it is progressive, a growing phase from the "milk stage" to the "meat stage," which is adulthood and full maturity in Christ.

Sanctification always requires the presence of God to produces His glory, which is the manifesting attributes of Himself. He transforms us from the worldly perspective and lifestyle by the renewing of our minds through the hearing and reading of the gospel, subsequently making us wise and leading us to growth in righteous attributes, so we produce good fruits and place the interests of God before the interests of self. Moreover, we live fully in Christ, basing our actions and attitude on biblical truths, yielding to God's directives, giving Him the rights, complete access, and control in our lives.

How does one achieve sanctification?

- By faith in Christ
- By obeying His commands
- By putting to death sin
- By submitting to God's discipline
- By the leading of the Holy Spirit of Christ
- By union with Christ's death and resurrection

The follower of Christ's role in sanctification is both passive and active. It is passive because we trust in Christ to sanctify us to God and active because we are responsible for doing and choosing that which is right and honorable unto God. Therefore, we must always pursue holiness, which reflects the nature of our holy God. We are set apart for His spiritual use and become vessels of honor separated from sin and holding firm to the truth of the gospel, according to biblical revelation. We must be desiring always to be useful to God with a sure and strong foundation rooted in Christ Jesus. Subsequently, we prepare for good works by demonstrating the virtues of the fruits of the spirit and living according to their principles (2 Timothy 2:21).

Sanctification is progressive or experiential. It is the calling of a person to obedience to the Word of God in his or her life. This is growing in Christ-like characteristics or spiritual maturity, which indicates that God has been working in his or her life and His Word has influenced him or her and is continually cleansing and purifying his or her life. Progressive sanctification is preventing sin from entering our lives daily so that we can have victory over sin, resulting in an ever-increasing growth experience as we constantly depend on Christ, abiding in Him and growing in spiritual maturity. Moreover, we walk in the spirit and draw near to Christ, yielding to righteousness, in obedient and faithful service and separation unto God.

Benefits of sanctification include the following:

- Growth in Christlikeness
- Growth in godliness
- Growth in good works
- Growth in obedience to His commands
- Growth in righteous attitude

Our willingness to live sanctified lives is what truly authenticates the power of Christ's death as it demonstrates Him living in us, for it requires us to be active in the process of sanctification by actively pursuing change. We should be putting off the old habits and putting on the Christ-like qualities of honesty, patience, and love with the leading of the Holy Spirit, ensuring that God's will be fulfilled in our lives. The Word of God is the embodiment of Christ that is used through the Holy Spirit to bring about change and sanctification in our lives from the inward to the external.

THREE

The Call to Obedience

BIBLICAL OBEDIENCE IS DEFINED AS accepting to obey God's authority by submissively yielding to His will and His commands. It is hearing God's Word and acting accordingly. It is a command from God to be obedient to Him, as it transforms us into His likeness and prepares us for union with Him in eternal glory, and it is an ongoing condition for salvation. Obedience is an important aspect of life, whether it is to God, in our homes, in our workplace, or in our community. It is compliance with an order, law, or authority. Hence, the command "to obey" is mentioned many times in the Holy Scriptures. In general terms, obedience is an act of submission to authority or compliance with an order or command.

Obedience is an essential part of the Christian faith, for it is choosing Christ and not self. The perfect model of obedience was Jesus Christ. He lived an obedient life while on earth. The scripture tells us, "He was obedient to death, even death on the cross" (Philippians 2:8). He was submissive to the will of His Father and embraced the suffering. Jesus said that if you are to be His disciples, you must first deny yourself, take up your cross, and follow Him, because the cross of Christ is a symbol of suffering, death, shame, and rejection. In being obedient to Christ by taking up our cross and following Him, we are denying ourselves and committing ourselves to a lifelong battle against sin, war against Satan, and humiliation from the world. Basically, this means being willing to die to self to obey and follow Christ (Mark 8:34).

Obedience to Christ and His righteous ways must be from the heart and not based on a defined standard of teaching or apostolic instructions. Rather, we are to walk in obedience with God by obeying His Word and the leadings of the Holy Spirit. Obedience is not optional, for we ought to be genuine, as it is an essential aspect of saving faith, which comes from our love for God. In our human state, it would be impossible to obey God's commands consistently. Hence, He promised His love, grace, and inward presence to help us to be obedient. As a result, He comes to those who are obedient through the workings of the Holy Spirit and make known the personal presence of Christ, so we can love God in our obedience and seek His honor and glory in this world.

Obedience is important for the following reasons:

- It is an act of worship
- It is better than sacrifice

- It brings blessings
- It is a command from God

The prophet Samuel tells us "To obey God is better than sacrifice" (1 Samuel 15:22), which means when we obey God's Word with our whole heart, it is better than any form of outward worship, service, or personal sacrifice. Consequently, God values obedience to Him highly. It is what He desires for us, His true followers, as it is evidence that shows if a person is truly of God. It is based on our love for Him, which exudes from a heart of gratitude for salvation received. Obedience is a command, and it is linked to love and joy; therefore, we obey God because of our love. We are told by God, "If you love Me, keep My commandments." To keep His commandments, you must first love Him. Love motivates obedience and is a key element in our relationship with Christ under the new covenant. It is critical in our daily walk of faith.

In the Old Testament, God called Joshua to lead His people into the Promised Land. However, for them to take possession of the Promised Land, they realized that it had to be maintained by faith in God, expressed in obedience to His Word. The Word of God is His commandments and revelation to Moses. It was the Israelites' central authority. They were to be faithful to God's Word by speaking about it, meditating on it, and obeying it fully. It's only by persevering in obedience to God's command and offering up the sacrifice of His covenant that Israel would continue as His treasured possession and God would fulfil His future purpose for Israel. To the New Testament followers, the possession of salvation is maintained by faith in Jesus Christ, which is expressed in obedience to His Word.

The Israelites were commanded to maintain their relationship with God by loving Him, obeying His voice, and responding in love, gratitude, and loyalty to Him so that they can know and enjoy Him. God also set before the people of Israel the choice to receive His blessing or a curse. For if they would obey His Word and separate themselves from the sins of the nations, then His blessing would be upon them. However, if they chose to remain in their sinful ways, God's curse of judgments would come upon them. Today, that same premise applies to us as followers of Christ; we can choose God's blessings or His curse. If we choose to obey Him and follow Christ, then we will receive His gift of salvation and escape the coming judgment (Deuteronomy 28).

Here are some blessings God promised to Israel.

- Prominence
- Provision
- Protection
- Prosperity
- Set apart
- Success

It is the duty of followers of Christ to obey Him faithfully, yielding and submitting to His will so we can hear His voice and receive His blessings. Our obedience first and foremost must be unto God in an intimate relationship, which includes faithfulness to the truth and the principles of His Word. We ought to be obedient and faithful to the pastors and teachers of the Word with a higher emphasis on loyalty to God. Also, we ought to be obedient to the visible church and godly leaders if they remain faithful and loyal to God, His Word, and the missions of the church. This form of obedience is important for spiritual revival and our hunger and desire to know and please God.

Obedience to God transforms us into His likeness and prepares us for union with Him in eternal glory, as it requires a personal relationship and faithfulness to Him, which are essentials for pleasing Him. Christ's followers who are obedient to Him are a testimony of holiness and a strong witness to the world, for they glorify God and demonstrate confidence in their eternal hope that they truly know and belong to Him. No one on earth will be perfect in obedience to God. Nevertheless, our desires must be submitted to the Lordship of Christ, and it will be expressed in our actions, words, and thoughts.

How do you show obedience to God?

- Abide in Christ
- Allow the Holy Spirit to control your life
- Love God with all your heart
- Surrender your life to Jesus Christ
- Trust in God's Word

Obeying God pulls us closer to Him as we grow and mature in the faith. Equally, the Holy Spirit of Christ teaches us more about His precepts, love, and faithfulness as we continue walking in obedience to Him. Jesus emphatically taught that being obedient to God and carrying out His will was the condition for entering the kingdom of God, because obedience to Him is an ongoing condition of salvation. God's grace always makes possible obedience, and what He demands for us is ascribed to His redemptive action. If there is no real obedience to God, then the fullness of the Holy Spirit is invalid, for the spirit in all His power is given only to those living in obedience. Obedience is not something we learn in a day; rather, it is a lifelong process that we pursue daily. It's putting into practice everything we've learned from God's Word and the Holy Spirit. Obedience is a response to God's very nature, which leads to a fulfilling life and thus experiencing His joy and peace.

The key to obedience is total submission to God. If our heart and mind are submitted to Him, it becomes natural because of our love for Him. In obeying God's command, we remain in His love and care. God held Abraham in high esteem as a model of obedience to the faith. Abraham sincerely endeavored to keep the laws and commandments of God. His faith was accompanied by obedience and trust, and God blessed him. Abraham had to make a sincere effort to please God through an obedient life to receive the covenant blessings. Subsequently, God specifically informed Isaac that the blessing of the covenant would be passed on to him if he continued to obey and keep His commands (Genesis 26:1-5).

The obedience that God expects from His people is not perfection but a sincere and earnest desire to obey Him. However, because of the weakness of human nature, we tend to fall at times, which indicates that we cannot live an obedient life in our own strength; instead, we must live by faith and trust in the Holy Spirit, for by faith, we learn to obey God and enjoy all His blessings. Faith produces obedience. Without it, we would not experience salvation. Furthermore, the Word of God is the means to obedience.

We hear, believe, and then act in obedience to the Word, which displays the glory of God in the lives of His people.

Here is why we must obey God:

- It is a command from Him
- It leads to a fulfilled life
- It leads to salvation
- It renews the mind
- It shows love and gratitude to Him

It is our responsibility to be obedient to God. We also have a resource to obey Him, which is God, who is in us both to will and to work for His good pleasure. Equally, He gives us His will, which is the desire to be obedient, and His power to work for His good pleasure. God's will and His power are the supernatural resources for obedience. Those resources are in the form of the Holy Spirit, who generates the desire and ability to obey God. Obedience is doing what God says, how He says, and when He says. It is impartial and requires our active choice. The grace of God is our basis for obeying God, since we all have violated His commandments and law; hence, obedience brings glorification to Him.

Faithfulness comes out of obedience to God, for we hear His voice and see His plans for our lives, and likewise, it strengthens our faith and gives us the ability to overcome temptations. Jesus, while being tempted by Satan, demonstrated perfect obedience as He kept and spoke the commandments of God, and consequently Satan fled from Him. Contrast that with Adam and Eve in the garden of Eden. Satan tempted them by quoting scripture from the Word of God and putting a twist on the truth, and Adam and Eve fell prey to Satan's lies instead of trusting in God and living by His Word. Jesus chose to trust in God and His Word, thus He successfully resisted Satan, giving us an example of how to resist and overcome Satan's temptations. This teaches us a valuable lesson that the more we grow in love and knowledge of God's Word in its entirety, the better we can identify sin and temptation and defeat Satan (Matthew 4:1–11).

Obedience to God protects us from the following:

- Doubt about salvation
- Loss of heavenly rewards
- Satan's entrance into our lives
- Sin and its consequences

True followers of Christ must always continue to be obedient to the Word of God for spiritual growth, to know Him, love Him, and have an intimate relationship with Him so they can experience the highest joy and peace every day. Our obedience comes from the heart and trusting in God because He has done so much for us. It shows that He is valuable and deserves our loyalty, praise, and honor, and it serves as a witness to God and the gospel. We display obedience to God, acknowledging that He is the supreme ruler of the heavens and earth, testifying of the truthfulness of His Word by "not" being just hearers of the Word but also "doers" of the Word, thus living in accordance with its standards.

Benefits of obedience to God include the following:

- Experiencing eternal joy, peace, and happiness
- Having a more intimate relationship with Him

- Having the leading of the Holy Spirit
- Hearing and knowing His voice
- Knowing the will of God for your life

Obedience unlocks the blessings of God in our lives. Every time we are obedient to God, His inner peace and joy flows in abundance through our hearts, and we know that we are in the center of His will, giving us the assurance of His blessings. Interestingly, the more we demonstrate our obedience to God, the more we will eventually glorify Him as our light shining in the world. One example is in the story of three Hebrew boys. God was glorified in their obedience to His Word for not bowing to the image of the golden King Nebuchadnezzar. Instead, they boldly witnessed to their allegiance to the one true, living God, and the manifestation of Jesus Christ in the form of the fourth man appeared in the fiery furnace. King Nebuchadnezzar said the fourth man was like the "Son of God." He then blessed the God of the three Hebrew boys, and he made a decree that anyone who spoke anything against the God of the three Hebrew boys would be killed. The three Hebrew boys were obedient to God and His Word, and as a result, the king promoted them in His kingdom (Daniel 3:1–30).

How does one learn obedience?

- Accept God's correction
- Meditate on God's Word
- Trust in God
- Wait on God
- Walk by faith

In the Bible, we are told that "Jesus learned obedience" by what He suffered (Hebrews 5:8). Jesus, the divine Son of God, as a human, experienced what it meant to obey God when He endured unpleasant and intense suffering in the garden of Gethsemane. As He prayed to God the Father in agony and tears, He received God's grace and help to undergo the appointed time of suffering, which was the cross. Jesus, through this process, chose to be obedient despite the difficulties, to fulfil the will of His Father. He was qualified to bring mankind eternal salvation. The nature of Jesus Christ helped Him to fully understand and relate to our struggles as humans. He did not disobey His Father; rather, He performed the duties required by God for the forgiveness of sins.

The first act of disobedience was with Adam and Eve when they refused to follow God's instructions of not eating from the tree of the knowledge of good and evil. Disobedience to God is not having respect for God, His law, and His word. It is caused by distrust in God and rebellion against Him. Disobedience always leads to God's judgment and punishment, as it is a sinful act against Him. It also leads to spiritual, physical, emotional, and psychological consequences for those who rebel against God, choosing to yield to self-will rather than surrender to God and His Will. Importantly, just as obedience is a choice, so too is disobedience, and those who choose to disobey God are enslaving themselves to sin and craving their sinful nature.

Why do people disobey God?

- They are unregenerated people

- They cannot understand or accept God's grace
- Satan has blinded their eyes

Disobedience to God begins in the heart of mankind as they refuse to be humble and submissive to God, thus demonstrating self-pride and arrogance in their behavior, not having any form of love for Him. Such an attitude toward God puts mankind at odds with Him, which could possibly destroy their entire future if they do not realize and resolve it quickly, as it can incur the wrath or the chastisement of God. We find in the Holy Scriptures the story of King Saul, who disobeyed and rebelled against God and His commands. Because of his rebellion, he was disqualified and rejected by God from being king of Israel. Additionally, he was given over to an evil spirit and demonic influences (1 Samuel 15:1–35).

To get the best in our lives, we must be obedient to God. He is omniscient, and though we cannot see Him, we must trust in His Word and commands, for He is all knowing, and His knowledge encompasses all the knowledge of this world. Obedience to God is a requirement for living righteously. Without obedience, mankind cannot attain the righteousness of Christ. We obey God because of our love for Him. It is a matter of duty; hence we serve Him in humility and genuine love. Obedience to God leads people to Him, to experience a fulfilled life in Christ, His love, and our hope of one day reigning with Christ in heaven.

The greatest and first commandment in the Holy Scriptures is "thou shall love the Lord thy God with all thy heart, soul and mind" (Matthew 22:37). This love is a devoted love. It's loving God in obedience and public identification with Him even in our suffering for His name's sake. True followers of Christ must be genuine and sincere in their love for God, as it is an essential aspect of grace. The grace of God comes to us freely; however, grace carries with it the obligation to obey God. Obedience to God is both possible and profitable. Therefore, we must strive to perfect obedience by living out God's Word in our deeds and actions. That is expressed in righteous standards, desiring His presence and fellowship with Him amid this evil and corrupt world.

Perfecting Holiness

The foundation of holiness is that there is only one God, one faith, and one baptism. There is only one way, and that is the way of holiness. Thus God commands us to be holy. The term *holy* describes the characteristics of God, which means that He is pure, clean, perfect, and infallible, and He has no flaws. Holiness never had a beginning, and it has no end. It's from everlasting to everlasting. God's nature is a spirit, and His spirit is Holy. Therefore, He is the Holy Spirit. Holiness comes from the one and only holy God. Holiness is the ways and characteristics of God, and within holiness is the doctrine, teaching, rules, regulations, and judgment of God. Holiness started before the foundation of the world. We are called to be holy. Holiness is the eternal attribute of God, for He is Holy. God's holiness is His first and foremost quality. It will never change. He is absolute in righteousness and His holiness, including His dedication to carrying out His purpose and plan for all humanity. His almighty power and eternal existence ensure that His holiness will triumph over all evil in this world.

The call to holiness is based on the character of God,

who is holy. It refers to the element itself, for it is the nature and quality of being holy. It must be actively pursued and cultivated into a lifestyle of holiness. Holiness is the condition of being set aside for service and worship to God. It is the result of obedience to God's law and commandments. Importantly, it is the teachings of the holy scriptures, and following its precepts is what makes you holy and blessed. It is a cooperative effort between God's spirit and ours, for only the spirit of God can put to death the things of the flesh; therefore, holiness is the state or attitude of the heart in devotion to God, who controls and directs our lives away from sin. Subsequently, the scripture tells us blessed and holy is he who hath a path in the first resurrection, indicating that only those who are holy will enter heaven (Ephesians 1:4, Revelation 20:6).

In essence, holiness is God's priority for His people. It was His purpose for us when He planned our salvation in Jesus Christ. Holiness is more than a lifestyle because holiness is the character of God, and it is His function and work. God's holiness is absolute perfection with no trace of sin. It embodies the mystery of His awesomeness. No one can be compared to Him, for His holiness pervades and shapes all His attributes, such as His love, mercy, wrath, and judgment, which are all holy. God is separated from all created beings and is absolute in purity, sinlessness, and holiness. His holiness is the first and foremost quality that is praised, for it is an eternal attribute of His, and it will never change. The highest characteristic of God that was revealed to the prophet Isaiah was that God's holiness signified His purity of character. He is separated from sin and is in opposition to all that is evil (Isaiah 6:3).

Holiness is defined as follows:

- The character of God
- The intelligence of God
- The teachings of God
- The thinking of God
- The standards of God
- The ways of God

Holiness is separation from sin and evil with a commitment to righteousness, for it carries the thought of being separated from the ungodly ways of the world. Holiness is the goal and purpose of our election in Christ, which refers to God choosing those whom He destined to be holy and blameless in His sight, dedicated, loving, and pleasing to Him. The election of mankind occurs only in union with Jesus Christ, for He has chosen us in Him. Jesus was the first elected of God. This is what God said about Jesus Christ: "Behold my servant, whom I have chosen; my beloved, in whom my soul is well pleased"(Matthew 12:18). Jesus, as the elected, is the foundation of our election, because it's only in union with Christ that we become members of the elect, for no one can come to Christ apart from union with Him through faith.

Holiness is a way of life. It causes change and institutes stability. Sometimes, it's difficult, but God requires us to be holy. Holiness must be evident in everything we do or say, for it is the aspect of our conduct and behavior, desiring the things that God delights in and living as He requires us to live, to be holy as He is holy. Holiness is the purpose of God and His will for His people. We are called to be blameless before Him, viewing life with the return of Jesus Christ in mind and not be caught up in sin. In considering Christ's return, our biblical standard must be unblameable in holiness. We must be wholeheartedly committed to God and separated from all that offends Him because we are His representatives. Holiness cannot be attained in our fleshly state; rather, our pursuit of holiness must include daily confessions of sin and seeking the help of the Holy Spirit to enable us to live holy lives.

God is holy and righteous. It impossible for Him to lie. Holiness is the intelligence of God as He relates His divine will, thoughts, standards, statutes, rules, regulations, and doctrine and reveals it to His servants, the prophets. Then God moved on them to write what was revealed to them and leave it for our learning. These prophets took on God's character; thus He called them holy prophets. Holiness is when people reflect the characteristics of God. To reflect God's character, you must be among God's Word so you can take on God's nature, but before you can take on God's nature, you must first be exposed to Him. Mankind must strive to overcome the darkness that is in self by allowing God's Word, along with His Holy Spirit, to transform them from unholy to holy. Being centered around God's holy precepts, commandments, law, and then holiness will gradually form and create you to be the man or woman that God wants.

Everything that's connected to God is holy:

- Holy apostles
- Holy faith
- Holy people
- Holy prophets

- Holy scriptures
- Holy Spirit

God's purpose for the children of Israel as His chosen people was to bring them out of Egypt to be a kingdom of priests and a holy nation, likewise the new covenant believers are called to be kingdom priests, separated from the world, and walk in God's righteousness and holiness. As God's chosen people, He gave the children of Israel instructions concerning what is clean and unclean food to help them remain a people separated from the ungodly society and remain holy. The same principles embodied in those instructions are still relevant today. Followers of Christ must distinguish themselves from certain surroundings, what they eat or drink or even how they dress. They must reject the unholy social customs of unbelievers, for they must be holy in all manners that portray Christ. As a result, God should be the sole source and standard for all our moral or spiritual conduct to live holy lives (Leviticus 11:44).

In the Old Testament, the holiness of God was manifested in the deliverance of the people of Israel from Egypt and the manifestation of His glory on Mount Sanai. Therefore, being holy for the people of Israel was based on their gratitude for the redemptive work of God that He accomplished on their behalf. It is important to note that the Mosaic Law was given to the people of Israel as God's standard of holiness, which was based on their obedience to the law, for they were to be holy as God is holy. Jesus Christ came to earth and lived under the law. He kept the law and manifested the holiness of God to mankind. He said, "Think not that I am come to destroy the law or the prophet; but to fulfil" (Matthew 5:17).

Why is holiness God's priority?

- He purposed it from before the beginning of time
- He purposed it in giving the Holy Spirit
- He purposed it in making a new creation
- He purposed it in sending Christ to earth
- He purposed it when Christ died on the cross
- He purposed it when He planned salvation

Holiness is the way of God; thus, He commanded us to be holy, for without holiness, no man can see God. Holiness helps us to follow, submit, and learn His teachings and how He wants all to be done; therefore, those who strive to be holy must be sound, so they will not easily be moved. As holy kingdom priests of God, we have direct access to Him through Jesus Christ. We are obligated to live holy lives, offer up spiritual sacrifices, such as our obedience, praise, service, and performance of good work, and present our bodies as an instrument of righteousness. God accepts our spiritual and jubilant worship of thanksgiving when it's accompanied by an inward disposition of reverence and purity of heart, with an earnest desire to be near Him. This is the aim of our redemption, being delivered from sin, having the spirit of holiness, which is the Holy Spirit indwelling our lives and helping us to achieve holiness.

God accepts and appreciates that which takes possession of His fellowship as He commands us to be holy for "I am Holy." He wants His people to have holiness by yielding themselves to His will, so He can sanctify us wholly to follow and perfect holiness. In pursuit of holiness, we must have the fear of God, hate sin and unrighteousness, and cleanse ourselves inwardly and outwardly from any defilement of the flesh with the Word of God, preserving our entire body, soul, and spirit to be blameless before God. We must continue holding on to Christ's unchanging hands, live in fellowship with Him, be fervent in prayer, and be separated from false doctrine and the religious system of this world.

Followers of Christ are made holy by the sanctifying work of the Holy Spirit as Christ indwells our lives and also through the power of the cross, which delivers us from the powers of sin. We have an infusion of God's grace to obey Him according to His Word and are renewed in the image of Christ daily. God then rewards us by drawing near with His protection, blessing, and fatherly care, loving and cherishing us as His children.

The pursuit of holiness does not end when we repent of our sins, accept Jesus Christ into our lives, and are baptized. Rather, it's just the beginning stage of becoming holy. Holiness must be active and pursued, as God expects us to cultivate a lifestyle of holiness. We must live according to His doctrine and the directives of the Holy Spirit because in perfecting holiness, we must increase spiritual maturity daily, thus being dead to sin and becoming vessels of righteousness. We glorify God, live in freedom from sin, and display His nature. We must develop spiritual fruits and refuse to revert to our former lifestyle; instead, we become the honorable vessels useful to God in His kingdom. Importantly, for holiness to be present in our lives, we are to participate in God's work by yielding to His will. It is His ultimate desire for us, His followers, to be holy and conformed into the image of His Son, Jesus Christ.

Attributes of holiness include the following:

- It brings peace and contentment
- It demonstrates love for God and others
- It is a powerful witness of God
- It prepares us for heaven
- It produces the fruits of the spirit

Followers of Christ are called to be holy, different, and separated from all other people. This separation is so that we might persevere in faith and godly love, loving God with an undivided heart in holy worship and devotion to Him. Holiness is an absolute necessity and a discipline for us as followers of Christ. It is powerful and practical, active, and not passive, nor is it just a state of the mind, as holiness is always connected to an individual's lifestyle and way of living. Our life should mirror the reflection of Christ. We should be living uprightly and in a godly way, in self-control and brotherly love, and being compassionate, thereby embracing the realities of what God requires of us and following Him continually, unconditionally, and unapologetically. We should become an imitation of Christ to the world, for He is holy, and what is true of Him must be true of His people; hence, we remain fervently committed to resist all that offends His very nature.

The key to living holy lives is understanding God's grace, which is given through Jesus Christ, and remembering His sacrifice on the cross. Furthermore, for anyone to exhibit holiness, it must come because of a right relationship with God. Apart from Him, it is impossible to be holy, for it is the indwelling of the Holy Spirit, filling and helping us to be holy. Therefore, we must be humble, being aware of our forgiveness, and be diligent in destroying any trace of sin that may enter our lives. Moreover, we are serious in our pursuit of pleasing God and holiness, thereby striving to never compromise ourselves with unholy things or activities. In truly understanding God's holiness, no one can remain the same, for it changes our way of thinking toward Him and compels us to recognize the need for change because without holiness, we would *not* be useful to God.

In the book of Revelation, we see four beasts praising God, saying, "Holy, holy, holy Lord God Almighty who was, and is to come"(Revelation 4:8). This demonstrates to us the supremacy of God, who will never change, for He is transcendent and unique in His greatness. The four-beast proclaimed that God is holy in all His ways, and His eternal existence ensures that His holiness will triumph over all evil in this world and the universe. Isaiah the prophet received a vision from God that revealed God's glory, majesty, and holiness, which demands those who serve Him be holy. In the vision, Isaiah saw seraphim, or angels, crying out, "Holy, holy, holy is the Lord of hosts." The earth is filled with His glory. Isaiah, in view of God's holiness, realized his own sinfulness and uncleanness and was afraid. God then cleansed his mouth and heart and made Isaiah fit to remain in His presence and be a servant and a prophet of God. It is important to note that it is only after God cleanses Isaiah that He commissioned Isaiah to be a prophet, which is a clear indication that for anyone to approach God or do work for His kingdom, his or her sins must be forgiven and his or her heart cleansed by His holy spirit (Isaiah 6:1-3).

Requirements to remain holy include the following:

- Apply God's Word in our lives daily
- Be obedient to God's Word
- Be dead to sinful desires
- Control the eyes and ears
- Glorify God daily
- Keep the mind on heavenly things

Basically, holiness is a faith to live by. It is not just a lifestyle; hence, the scripture tells us to "build up ourselves on our most holy faith" (Jude 1:20). Moreover, holiness counteracts the way we used to think of ourselves and our outlook on life, the world, and the self because the way to be holy unto God is simply through obedience. Therefore, to be holy, you must first be obedient unto God, for it is the centerpiece and bedrock of holiness. To learn holiness is to know God through His Word because nothing reflects Him better than His Word. Hence, in perfecting holiness, there is an ongoing process that requires complete surrender of our will to the will of God and the leading of the Holy Spirit, for in one's own self, holiness is unattainable.

Furthermore, we must pray without ceasing daily, seeking the help of the Holy Spirit as we make a covenant with our eyes and ears to prevent impurities from entering our souls by way of these two senses. We must consecrate our minds by renewing our thoughts and placing our focus on God. Be committed to memorizing scriptures to help in times of trouble, hiding God's Word in your heart daily. Satan, the enemy of our souls, is seeking to destroy our lives at any given opportunity; hence, we must always be on the alert to counteract his strategies by knowing areas in our life that are weak and strengthening them by cultivating a deep love for God and a desire to know Him in a more intimate way.

Exhibiting Godliness

Godliness is one of the seven virtues listed in the Holy Scriptures. It is defined as belief in God and reverence for His character and law. It is the product of following the truth of God's Word, as it always results in obedience to the truth. The seven virtues speak to the quality of our character, moral excellence (being a morally good person), and spiritual excellence. God has given us these virtues; therefore, we must sincerely endeavor to add to our faith godly characteristics to grow in our lives. Knowledge of the truth of God's Word leads to godliness. Hence, we ought to train ourselves to be godly and pursue godliness in Christ, not just the outward practice of godliness, for the scripture tells us "Godliness with contentment is great gain"(1 Timothy 6:6). Godliness has value for all things, as it holds to the promises of God for this present life and the next life to come. Godliness is the foundation on which godly characters are built and executed (2 Peter 1:6).

Godliness expresses the fear of God and the love of God with an attitude of deep respect for Him. It means yielding always to the Holy Spirit of Christ. It's an attitude that permeates all the Christian virtues. With a mind set on spiritual matters, we actively seek to develop a spiritual relationship with God. Godliness is a positive way of life that is influenced by God and a reflection of the Christian faith, as it has the qualities of virtue, knowledge, patience, and genuine thankfulness. It is the wellspring of gratitude and leads to growth in godliness. The apostle Paul tells us the grace of God teaches His followers to say no to ungodliness and to live in self-control, uprightness, and godliness, which is the purpose of saving grace and salvation. We are to decisively reject the ungodly passions, pleasures, and values of this world and live righteous and godly lives while awaiting our blessed hope, the return of Jesus Christ.

Here are the seven qualities to add to our faith:

- Brotherly love
- Charity or love
- Godliness
- Knowledge
- Patience
- Temperance
- Virtue

The scripture speaks of the mystery of godliness. It was once hidden but has now been revealed to us by God. It is Jesus Christ, the Son of God, becoming flesh. Jesus Christ was manifested in the flesh so humanity can visibly see and identify Him as the Son of God, to destroy the works of Satan, and to provide us with a model for how to live godly lives. He was seen and announced by the angels, preached about among the nations, believed on in the world, vindicated by the spirit, and taken up to heaven in glory. This mystery of godliness involves a declaration of spiritual truth that is revealed in the Word of God, through divine inspiration concerning our biblical faith.

Subsequently we respond to the things of God in faith, which in turn, produces obedience and godly living (1 Timothy 3:16).

In the scriptures, we find all things that pertain unto life and godliness, such as love for God, salvation through Jesus Christ, Christ's intercession on our behalf, the baptism and indwelling of the Holy Spirit, and communication with other believers. All those elements are what followers of Christ need for life and godliness because no additional human wisdom, technique, or theory can complete the sufficiency of God's Word. True devotion to God stems from the fear of Him, which draws our hearts to worship, honor, and reverence. We are to be in awe of Him, prompting us to live godly lives and view God in His infinite majesty as the creator and supreme ruler of the universe. Godly living is cultivated when a follower of Christ forms an intimate relationship with God and grows because of his or her actions, behavior, and conduct. God is preparing us to be with Him one day in heaven (2 Peter 1:3).

How does one develop in godliness?

- Having an intense prayer life
- Having the indwelling of the Holy Spirit
- Loving God
- Receiving the gift of salvation
- Studying the Word of God

By faith, Enoch walked with God in great intimacy and undoubtedly excelled in godliness. He lived by faith in God, trusted in God's Word and promises, and endeavored to live a holy life, well pleasing unto God. He cried out against ungodliness and immorality by warning the people of his generation of God's coming judgment and the punishment for their ungodly deeds that they had committed. Enoch embraced God's ways by walking faithfully with God while standing firm against the ungodliness of his generation; thus his life was a message of godliness, and for his faithfulness, God honored him by taking him from the earth without him experiencing death. Followers of Christ today must emulate Enoch's life as a model of how to live godly lives in this world, by denouncing sin, winning souls for Christ, and warning humanity of the judgments of Jesus Christ and His imminent return (Genesis 5:21–24).

Godliness refers to a person's active response to the things of God. It then leads to obedience to God and godly living, based on knowing His truth, the awareness of His sovereignty, and the manifesting power of the Holy Spirit controlling our desires and enabling us to resist ungodly influence. Therefore, we bring all our desires and thoughts in alignment with God's will and the leading of the Holy Spirit, having the assurance that God will help us as we sincerely endeavor to live godly lives. Consequently, we surrender our all to Jesus Christ, study His Word, be obedient to His commands, and fellowship with others in Christ, thereby reflecting the heart, wisdom, and very nature of Christ while here on earth. No longer do we try to please only the self; instead, it is all about pleasing God and striving toward godliness, subsequently knowing and understanding the things of the spirit and seeing life from a different perspective.

The following are six pieces of evidence of a godly person:

- They are devoted to God's Word
- They have a constant prayer life
- They have genuine love for God
- They hope in God
- They show gratitude to God and others
- They trust God totally

Followers of Christ have a duty to live a holy and godly life, as it is considered a privilege. We are spiritually blessed in heavenly places in Christ Jesus because God is the provider of every good thing or gift, as seen in creation. When He finished creating everything, He repeatedly stated, "It is good." The Holy Scriptures tells us that "nothing will He withhold from them that walk uprightly." This is directed specifically at us as followers of Christ who are living godly and righteous lives. Hence, we continue to fulfil His purpose in our lives by walking with and trusting in Him to help us finish the task, whether it be physically, spiritually, temporally, or eternally. God will bless us with all things good so that we can accomplish our mission here on earth for His glory. All God's blessings seen, or unseen, are good. He has blessed us in Jesus Christ, whom He raised from the dead and who is now seated at the right hand of God interceding on our behalf. Through Jesus Christ, we receive God's spirit, wisdom, revelation, and knowledge concerning His redemptive purpose for the present and future salvation. He also gives us more abundant power from the Holy Spirit to help us perfect godliness (Psalm 84:11).

In growing in godliness, we are motivated to persevere in the process, being assured that God has called and chosen us as His very own; hence, it requires diligence, effort, hard work, and discipline, as it's the only way to remain in God's grace. Subsequently, we begin to trust God and His gracious promises as we cultivate godly qualities, walk closely with Him, seek to know Him better, and endeavor to please Him, while safeguarding ourselves from falling away from the faith. The importance of having the right motivation for growing in godliness is our desire to bring glory unto God by which His grace is demonstrated in and through our lives and manifested as we grow spiritually in godly relationship, brotherly love, kindness, and genuine love for God and others.

Benefits of growing in godliness include the following:

- Assurance of our salvation
- Complete knowledge of God
- Eternal blessings
- Eternal peace
- Fruitfulness
- Heavenly focused mind
- Perseverance

Godliness is an external behavior that is continually seeking after the heart of Christ. Furthermore, it's being devoted to growing spiritually and deepening our faith by glorifying God, sharing the gospel, and being ambassadors for Him. In considering such privilege, in godliness and humility, we honor God with a clear conscience for His great power within, which enables us to do good work for Him, being strengthened as He gives to us the motives, principles, and direction and influences our conduct. In growing in godliness, we experience the satisfaction of knowing that our lives are fruitful in the light of God and eternity, knowing that God has called and chosen us. Jesus teaches us in scripture, that all God's faithful people who are living godly and holy lives are of great worth to Him, for He values us and our needs, and He treasures our faithfulness, love, and loyalty as we bring honor and glory to His name here on earth.

People who are not growing in godliness are being blinded from the truth of God's Word, what Christ has done for them, for they are not truly saved. This may be because of following false teaching or preaching, or they may have fallen completely away from the faith because of doubt or unbelief; hence, they will live useless and unfruitful lives. False religion and preachers allow believers to indulge in serious acts of sin. They also teach pardon for sin but not the imperatives of godliness and holiness. Instead, they pervert the grace of God and deny Jesus Christ as the only way to God. People who follow these false religious doctrines are shortsighted and have forgotten that their old sins have been forgiven. Instead, they focus more on their present circumstances, thus allowing their motivation to grow in godliness to be quenched as they slowly drift far away from God (2 Peter 1:9).

Ungodliness is a condition of being polluted by sin, actively opposing God in disobedience, which is caused by the acts of the flesh and the desires of the world. The ungodly are people who represent the ways and counsel of the world. They do not abide in God's Word. They are cynical about God and mockers of that which is holy, for they are not in agreement with the things of God. The psalmist tells us, "The ungodly is like a chaff that the wind blows away" (Psalm 1:4). This means that these people are powerless against God's judgments, for they are separated from Him, thus having no part in His kingdom. Rejection of God's law and despising His Word will only result in the ungodly people being given over to the consequences of their own sins and divine punishment.

The ungodly are described as follows:

- Blinded by sin
- Condemned by God
- Delighting in evil
- Like chaff
- Unrepentant
- Will perish for all eternity

In the beginning of the book of Psalms, we note that there are two types of people recognized by God. The godly, those who love God, live righteously, and are obedient to His Word separate themselves from the things of the world. The ungodly, these are unrepentant sinners, those who do not abide in God's Word, are the children of disobedience who delight in evil and the things of the world. Basically, the unrepentant sinners are children of the devil. It is important to note that the separation of these two types of people will exist throughout this earth and eternity. The people of God are known as children of the light, and the unrepentant people are of the devil and known as the children of darkness. It is imperative for mankind to choose wisely on whether to live godly lives by drawing life from God and prosper or live ungodly lives and be condemned by God on the day judgment.

Followers of Christ should not associate themselves with the ungodly because it can cause unrighteousness to be advanced in their lives and hinder their commitment to God, which can either be jeopardized or compromised. Followers of Christ are made into a new creation and belong to Christ, having the image of God. They share in His glory with a renewed knowledge and understanding of Him. Therefore they live godly lives. We ought to be mindful of our association with the ungodly. There is a distinct difference between the godly those whose root system draws from God and the ungodly who delight in sin and the counsel of the world. The only reason why followers of Christ should associate with the ungodly is attempting to win their souls for Christ by witnessing to them about God's grace, mercy, forgiveness, and salvation and warning them of the judgment of Christ.

FOUR

The Call to Oneness

SPIRITUAL ONENESS IS BELIEVING IN one God. God the Father is the one true, living God and not a pantheon of other gods. Therefore, He must be the sole object of our love, obedience, and glorification. Unity in Christ is a result of a person's maturity in the faith and in the knowledge of the Son of God; hence, we make every effort to maintain the unity of the spirit of Christ through the bond of peace. Oneness joins people together and is built on a solid purpose, which comes for the heart and soul, as it integrates the glory of God, His kingdom's purpose, and the manifestation of His power. In the Old Testament, the people of Israel were told "the Lord our God is one Lord," which teaches and affirms that God is the true, living God and is all-powerful among all other gods and spirits. Furthermore, the aspect of oneness served as the basis for prohibiting the worshiping of other gods. Rather, we are to fear God and serve only Him. The children of Israel were to have oneness in purpose, essence, mind, heart, and passion toward the Almighty God (Deuteronomy 6:4).

The New Testament followers of Christ ought to believe in one God who manifests Himself in His Son Jesus Christ. Jesus Christ was the manifestation of God in human form when He came to earth as the son of God, "God incarnate." He took on the form of man who acted as a veil and operated in the body of Jesus Christ. Hence, Jesus said, "If you see me, then you see my father." This is the mystery that the scripture speaks about. Followers of Christ must believe in the doctrinal truth of God and the oneness of God as revealed in His Word, being united in the same mind, having the same love, and living in harmony with one another. The Holy Spirit, which is God, helps us to have the spirit of oneness, in our hearts and minds in union with Christ. The glory of God is manifested in and through us so that the world can see Him.

Jesus, in His final prayer for His disciples, among all He desired, prayed "that they may be one" in purpose and fellowship, as demonstrated by Him and His Father. This unity that Jesus prayed for was not organizational unity but spiritual unity. He did not pray for His followers to become one; rather, it is that they "may be one," which is a continual oneness. Jesus prayed for those who are fully devoted to Him, His Word, and holiness to be spiritually unified in heart, purpose, mind, and will so that the world can see that He was sent by God. Importantly, if any of those factors of unity listed is missing, then the true unity that Jesus prayed for will not exist in our oneness with each other or in the body of Christ. Jesus's prayer of oneness is based on the disciples' common relationship to God, having the same attitude toward the Word of God and seeing the need to go out into the world and save the lost (John 17:20–25).

Spiritual oneness is based on the following:

- Desiring to bring salvation to the world
- Living in Christ
- Obedience to the Word of God
- Receiving and believing the truth of God's Word
- Sanctification
- Separation from the world

In Jesus's prayer, He emphasized the importance of oneness as He mentioned the word *one* four times: "that they all may be *one*, as the Father art in me; that they may be *one* in us; that they may be *one*, even as we are *one*" (John 17:21). This oneness involves our unity as followers of Christ. We are to have the same belief in the truth of the gospel in our words and actions. He prayed that the glory that God gave Him, He would give to us, His followers, and this glory is the path of holiness, humble service, and cross bearing. True unity of believers will lead to the true glory of God, for humility, self-denial, and willingness to suffer for Christ ensure true oneness. God desires us to live in harmony with one another, to be established in love, holiness, and unity in accordance with Him that together we may be unified with one voice glorifying and bringing honor to God.

Jesus not only prayed for the oneness of all followers of Christ, but He was also spiritually inspired to show us how we should pray for one another. We should be praying that others may know Christ and His Word; for God to keep them from falling prey to the world and Satan; that they may be holy in thoughts and deeds, persevere in the faith, and love Christ; and that His spirit may dwell in and with them. True followers of Christ must first be joined by the spirit of Christ and must be living by the spirit. The scripture tells us for by one spirit, we were baptized into Christ's body, uniting us in the body and making us spiritually one with other believers. Spiritual oneness among true followers of Christ can only be accomplished through God working within us with the help of the Holy Spirit so that our unity reflects the perfect unity, the oneness of the Father and the Son (1 Corinthians 12:13).

The palmist David expressed that same spiritual truth, as did the Apostle Paul, as he states "how good and pleasant it is for brethren to dwell together in unity" (Psalms 133:1), which is for us to be established in the same love, holiness, and oneness. He knows that unity is essential for us because the Holy Spirit would not operate if there were division based on selfish ambitions and sin, thus the importance of being perfectly joined together in the same mind and judgment. Furthermore, we must remain faithful to the Word of God, as it takes priority over loyalty to Christian institutes and traditions, individuals, or the visible church that has become unfaithful to Christ. Spiritual oneness or unity can only be maintained by being loyal to the truth of God's Word, by obeying its teachings and keeping in line with the Holy Spirit. There cannot be unity of the spirit apart from the affirmation that Jesus Christ is the ultimate authority for all followers of Christ, and His authority is communicated in the Word of God (1 Corinthians 1:10).

The true essence of oneness is defined as follows:

- Defending the gospel at all costs
- Faithfulness to the doctrine of God
- Living in a manner worthy of God
- Obedience to God and His Word
- Standing firm in one spirit and purpose

As followers of Christ, we are all given an important task of defending the gospel of Christ, defend biblical truth, and resisting those who distort the faith. Oneness in Christ involves love, forgiveness, and sacrifice; therefore, maintaining oneness in the faith must be based on an active love that seeks to resolve problems, reconcile differences, and inspire mutual loyalty and obedience to God and His Word. Any attempt to maintain oneness or unity must never invalidate the Word of God or be based on the compromise of biblical truth. Rather, we ought to be spiritually mature, speaking the truth of God's doctrine in love, with our love firstly directed to Christ, the church, and one another. Importantly, spiritual oneness cannot be achieved by the flesh or through human efforts or organization, for this is considered a betrayal of the unity for which Jesus Christ prayed.

Sin is a disruptive force that creates division, separation, doubt, and constant fighting in our lives; however, salvation brings together the followers of Christ and restores the unity that God created in the beginning of creation between mankind and Himself. This oneness cannot be produced, for it is living and vital to the Christian walk with Christ, as unity of the followers of Christ and the spirit begins within and is expressed outwardly. When we are in union with Christ by the spirit of baptism, we become members of the body through the regenerative power of the Holy Spirit, thereby making us a part of the body of Christ, for God's purpose and our calling in Him, which is to be His disciples and be of service to Him in the ministry.

Here are the seven elements of oneness:

- One body
- One spirit
- One hope of our calling
- One lord
- One faith
- One baptism
- One God and Father of all

The scripture tells us that "everyone of us is given grace according to the measure of the gift of Christ" (Ephesians 4:7). Everyone who has accepted Jesus Christ as savior is a member of the body, for we are joined together in one common goal, which is to glorify God. No matter the diversity, we are one. This difference and diversity would contribute to and equip our ministries separately, as each part works together, thus creating a deeper and more mature unity in Christ. Oneness in Christ is a union that is established between us and Christ wherein everything that He is and has is shared with us, His followers. The only thing that cannot be shared with us is His deity. As members of the body, we belong to God and are in Him, so though many, we are "one body" in Christ and individual members of another, which makes up "one universal church".

Oneness in Body, Spirit, and Hope

There is only one church, and that is Jesus Christ *the rock*. He said, "Upon this rock, I will build my church and the gates of hell shall not prevail against it"(Matthew 16:18). This means that Christ built His church on the truth of God's Word and the confessions of His apostles that Jesus Christ is the Son of God. Jesus Christ is the Rock, the first foundation of the church. The apostle Peter also states that Jesus Christ is the living stone, a chief cornerstone, the stone that was disallowed by men but chosen by God and is precious. The church is presented as the people of God, the company of redeemed believers made possible by Jesus Christ's death, and our first function is to be in oneness in our living and personal relationship with God. The church is the Lamb's wife, and it must have the same doctrine with no division, for there is one standard church that possesses one people and one way to God (1 Peter 2: 4–5).

Here is what the church represents:

- The holy people called out of the world
- The body of Christ
- The bride of Christ
- The temple of God

Importantly, contrary to what many people believe, "the church" is not a building but people, the bodies of the followers of Christ, of which Jesus Christ is the head. The body of Christ "is the universal church" that was created in Jesus Christ of individuals whom He values, having God's grace, which sustains all ministry in Him. Jesus Christ came to earth in the likeness of man, and after His ascension, He continued His work in the world through His redeemed followers, "the church," who function as "the body of Christ." The church is the spiritual body of Christ, which has many members performing different functions; however, there is only one body, thus, the importance of the church being one, striving in spiritual unity, just as Jesus Christ and His Father are one. God appointed Jesus Christ to be head of all things, which includes the church, His body, and the fullness of Him. Importantly, the body of Christ is a holy entity that ought to be respected and treated with honor.

As members of Christ's church, we are called His true followers, and every member possesses a gift and is called to service within the body to build up, strengthen, and edify the body of Christ and carry out His purpose in the world. Within the content of spiritual equality of gifts, men and women are equal, created in their own image with their own assigned roles in Christ. That is why the people of God ought to remain one, reflecting unity in the bond of peace with each other. In being a part of the divine family of God, the seven elements of oneness must be evident in us as they display our unity in Him; however, those who lack any of those elements show a clear indication that they do not belong to God's family (Ephesians 4:1–7).

How do we build up the body of Christ?

- Be a witness for Christ in the world
- Be faithful to the doctrine of Christ
- Be genuine in love toward God and one another
- Be of service to God in our ministries
- Be of the same mind in Christ

- Be promoters of the truth of the gospel
- Be unified in the things of Christ

True members of the body of Christ display the genuineness of their faith, as their lives and actions are aligned with the teachings of the doctrine of God's Word. They are sure of their salvation and are in common bond with other members, regardless of their background or race. As equal parts of the body of Christ, we are actively serving God, sharing Him with others, and contributing to peace and unity within the body. Importantly, each member is placed in the body according to the will of God, and all members are important for the spirit's well-being and the proper functioning of the body. The body of Christ is the visible and spiritual manifestation of Christ, where we love, admire, and follow completely after Him, being loved and protected by Him, redeemed, justified, and created together by God in Christ Jesus.

The scripture tells us that "by one spirit are we all baptized into one body,"(1 Corinthians 12:13), which refers to the spirit baptizing believers into Christ's body, uniting them in the body and making them spiritually one with other believers. One spirit pertains to the unity provided by the Holy Spirit, which is the spirit of God, His power and presence, or the keeping of God. This unity of the spirit is created through our union in Jesus Christ and the joining of our life to Him as He then pours out His spirit upon all those who believe in Him. Subsequently, we feel His presence near, empowering us to do His will, for it creates in us the confidence that through Christ we are children of God, thereby making reality the truth that Christ loves us.

Oneness of the spirit is based on the sensitivity of Jesus Christ, for He is the one who brings the hearts of His followers together for the good of His kingdom, as the spirit of God binds our hearts in unity, something that the world cannot comprehend. Subsequently, followers of Christ are joined in "one spirit," not one soul, because the soul is the personality of a person and is used to express the union between our spirit and God's. The soul is natural and impure. Jesus Christ is the life-giving spirit; therefore, His union with His follower is with our spirit through our continual intimate communion with Him as the Holy Spirit indwells our lives.

Here are six ways to remain in oneness of the spirit:

- Always act in accordance with God's Word
- Always be in harmony with God's Word
- Always earnestly desire and value the manifestation of the spirit
- Always exhort others to persevere in the faith
- Always have an inward urging to do God's will
- Always put to death the misdeeds of the flesh

Oneness of the spirit is based on our loyalty, generosity, love, service, selflessness, and acceptance of one another in the body of Christ and of God's Word. We continue to faithfully proclaim and teach in the power of the spirit of Christ, thereby guarding and defending God's Word against all distortion and alteration. We are unified in one spirit, in the knowledge of the doctrine of Christ, thereby being matured in the faith so that we will not be blown away by winds of different doctrine. Instead, we are rooted firmly in the core principles and foundation of God's Word. Therefore, we would not be easily deceived. Followers of Christ united in one spirit find a new power within, a power that allows us to overcome sin, live righteously, and submit to the Holy Spirit's direction, which enables oneness among us by focusing our attention, energy, and thoughts on the things of God.

Followers of Christ united in one body and one spirit and living in accordance with God's Word automatically start becoming obsessed with an eternal hope that gives us power to live courageously in Christ and believe in heavenly realities. The scripture tells us that we ought to be in "one hope of our calling," which is the hope of Jesus Christ's second coming, where we will live and reign with Him forever in heaven, thereby trusting in the promises of God and what He says in His Word to be true. Our hope is confident expectation based upon the sure foundation of Jesus Christ for He is called our hope. He came to bring us hope, thus fulfilling all the messianic prophecies about Him in the scriptures. Consequently, Christ living within us is our assurance of our future glory and eternal life. Hence, in oneness, we hope in God for the present, and we are never alone, for He is always with us, and one day in the future, we will be with Him throughout all eternity (Romans 15:12–13, 1 Timothy 1:1).

Biblical hope is an indication of certainty, a firm confidence in God about the future that is based upon God's promises and revelation. It is inseparable with a firm faith and confident trust in God, for there is no doubt. It is reality, not a feeling, based on God's Word, His character, and the finished work of Jesus Christ. The scripture tells us "Hope maketh not ashamed because the love of God is shed in our hearts by the holy spirit" (Romans 5:5). This is the ever presence of God's love, which sustains and assures His followers of our hope for the future. As we continue living in one hope, the hope that our savior will soon return and take us out of this world to be ever present with Him, it is a major source of comfort. We are watchful and hopeful for His return.

The basis of our hope is the following:

- The fulfilment of God's promises
- The revelation of the new covenant
- The scriptural revelation of God's faithfulness
- The truth of God's Word

The apostle Peter tells us of our hope as he said, "Blessed be the God and Father of our Lord Jesus Christ, which according to His abundant mercy hath begotten us again unto a lively hope by the resurrection of Jesus Christ from the dead" (1 Peter 1:3). Therefore, followers of Christ must always put their hope in Christ, wait for Him, and remain in His Will, and He will watch over and protect us in this life. The hope of our calling is in common with all followers of Christ to be with God forever in glory, as our hope is strengthened by the Word of God and His love, which sustains us even in sufferings. The revelation of the new covenant in Christ Jesus gives us more confidence of our hope in God, as Jesus Christ destroyed the works of Satan. He drives out demons during His earthly ministry, demonstrating His power over Satan, and moreover, by His death and resurrection, He shattered the powers of Satan's realm and exhibited and elevated the powers of God's kingdom.

The sure hope for followers of Christ is our anchor amid life, for it derives from the very nature of Jesus Christ and God's Word; therefore, we continue in one hope as the spirit of Christ floods our hearts with His love. God is the God of hope, for He is the object and assurance of our hope. Therefore, as we go through life's struggles, He will fill us with all joy and peace through the power of the Holy Spirit so that we may abound in hope and His love. The psalmist tells us, "Happy is he that hath the God of Jacob for his help, whose hope is in the Lord his God"(Psalm 146:5). Therefore, it is imperative that we never place our confidence, trust, or hope in man, material possessions, or money, where there is no help, for they will all disappoint us. Rather we must put our trust, confidence, and hope on God, who is our helper and will never fail us.

Oneness in Christ involves the following:

- Belief in God's love and grace
- Belief in Jesus Christ's second coming to earth
- Belief in the completion of our salvation
- Belief in our eternal home
- Belief in our eternal life with Christ
- Belief in the resurrection of our immortal bodies
- Belief in our rewards and crown in heaven

Hope is an enduring virtue of the Christian life; it produces joy and peace within us through the power of the Holy Spirit. We know that our only hope of victory lies in us continually approaching the throne of grace through Christ, that we may receive the power of God and His grace in time of need. As followers of Christ, our hope brings eternal values, strength, faith, God's love, and praise unto Him, as it is a fundamental component of life, knowing that we will not be confounded or put to shame, being free from fear and anxiety. Moreover, we demonstrate more confidence in God, His protection, and His care as we continue to hope in Him and His promises, boasting in this hope and exhibiting great boldness in the faith as we exalt Christ in life and in death. In contrast, those who do not place their trust and belief in Jesus Christ as Lord and savior are without hope, thereby having no meaning to their very existence (Philippians 1:20, 2 Corinthians 3:12).

Oneness in the Lord, Faith, Baptism, and God

The scripture asserts that there is only "one Lord," which refers to Jesus Christ, through whom are all things and we by Him; this means that Jesus Christ has dominion over everything with the exemption of God the Father, who is over Him. The name *Lord* is significant to God, as He said, "I will publish the name of the Lord; ascribe ye greatness unto our God; He is the Rock; His work is perfect all His ways are judgement" (Deuteronomy 32: 3-4). Apart from God the Father and the Word of God, Jesus Christ as "one Lord" has greater Lordship, authority and power over all lords and gods of this universe. His role as "one Lord" is to exercise God's rule over all creation. God the Father entrusted all authority and all things to Jesus Christ, and because of this, salvation rested solely on Him, thereby through Him, His followers will experience true unity with each other, for Jesus Christ is the ultimate foundation (Matthew 28:18, 1Corinthians 8:6,).

Jesus Christ, as "One Lord," is shown by the following:

- His death, burial, and resurrection
- His declaration of Him by God as His Son
- His deity
- His divine names given to Him by God
- His divine worship and prayer addressed to Him
- His sinlessness and holiness

The name *Jesus* is an inherited name from God the Father. The scripture tells us that "by inheritance He obtained a more excellent name"(Hebrews 1:4). Christ is New Testament name for the Old Testament Messiah. It is the title of God, which means "Anointed One." God the Father exalted Jesus Christ in this earth and in heaven as "Lord and Christ." Jesus Christ is the firstborn of every created being, the first in position, the heir, and the ruler of creation as the eternal Son of God. He is also the firstborn from the dead, as He was the first to rise from the dead with a spiritual and immortal body. Jesus is known as Lord of lords because of His divine standing, and by Him being divine, He made atonement for the sins of the world. Jesus Christ as "one Lord" is the full and complete Godhead with all that it represents residing in Him (Philippians 2:9–11).

Humanity and everything in the universe are brought in unity and harmony under the control of Jesus Christ; however, not all people are reconciled to Him because some choose to reject Christ's offer of salvation. In the story where Jesus Christ wept over Jerusalem, He referred to Himself as

"Lord" when He directed two of His disciples to get a colt from the nearby village before He entered Jerusalem. Also, the palmist David exalted Jesus Christ as "my Lord" and the One on whom we must call for salvation. The word *Lord* means more than just master when referring to Jesus Christ, for it is a name that is superior to every name, a name that stands for His authority, holiness, mercy, love, and grace. This name declares that Jesus Christ is the full revelation of God to humanity. Jesus Christ is now exalted in heaven for He has the authority to pour out the Holy Spirit on His followers and intercede on our behalf (Luke 19:28–40).

Some divine offices assigned to Jesus Christ are the following:

- Bestower of resurrection life
- Giver of salvation
- Judge of all humanity
- Sustainer of all things

For followers of Christ, confession and unity in the knowledge that there is only "one Lord" is essential to the Christian faith, as they pledge their allegiance to Jesus Christ as the begotten Son of God, for His redemptive work as Lord of all and the Lord of glory. Jesus Christ's life was the light for everyone, and through Him, God's truth, nature, glory, and power are made available to all who believe in Him. For He illumines all who hear the gospel of Christ by imparting a measure of grace and understanding for us to freely accept or reject His message. Importantly, as "one Lord," His followers united must act toward Jesus Christ in the same manner as toward God the Father, for they are one, thereby believing in Him, worshiping Him, praying to Him, serving Him, and loving Him. Jesus Christ is our access to God, and His throne of grace is exclusively through Jesus Christ as our mediator and high priest, for we rely on His sacrificial death to cover our sins when we pray in faith (1 Timothy 2:5).

According to the Word, without faith, it is impossible to please God; therefore, for followers of Christ to be pleasing and acceptable to God, we must be united in "one faith" in the belief of the one true, living God without visibly seeing Him. An essential condition required for God's protection is that His followers be in one faith, so He can protect us against Satan's forces of evil that seek to destroy our salvation in Christ. The scripture tells us, "Through faith, we understand that the world was framed by the Word of God." Having "one faith" is an understanding whereby we obtain knowledge through our five senses and the knowledge of God in the spiritual realm, which only happens though revelation and understanding of God's Word through faith. Importantly, the natural mind cannot understand the things of God, including creation, for it's only a renewed mind in Christ that can comprehend such things (Hebrews 11:3, 6).

We learn from the scripture that "faith" is the substance of things hoped for, the evidence of things not seen," which indicates that faith is trusting in God in all situations, thus enabling His followers to persevere and remain steadfast and loyal to Him and His Word at all times. By having one faith in God, we believe in the existence of a personal, infinite, holy God who loves and cares for us. We believe that He is a rewarder to those who earnestly seek Him and enjoy His presence. Furthermore, we know the faith that God approves of is a faith that can surrender God's promises back to Him for their fulfilment according to His will. Moreover, believers hold on to those promises, and being in oneness of faith is given a distinct mark, which indicates that we belong to God. For He is our shield and our great reward henceforth. He will sustain us to the very end and eternity (Hebrews 11:1).

How do we demonstrate one faith in God?

- We believe in God's goodness
- We have confidence in His Word
- We obey God's commands
- We persevere in testing and trials
- We regulate life on God's promises
- We seek God daily

In having one faith, we are united with Jesus Christ, His nature, and the perfection of His work. This is a faith that saves so we can overcome the world, experience the power of God, motivate change, and enrich lives for the kingdom of God. Followers of Christ united in one faith have a triumphant faith that sees eternal realities. We must be loving Christ to such an extent that the world's sinful pleasures, ungodly ways, and materialism lose their attraction to us. Instead, we look at them with aversion and disgust. United in one faith, we manifest gratitude to and love for God as our oneness in faith is accompanied with love for each other and Christ because faith and love is inseparable. When we were born of God, the Holy Spirit poured the love of God into our hearts, which comforts us in our trials and temptations, thus bringing Christ's presence ever so near (1 John 5:4).

One faith is proclaiming what Jesus Christ did for humanity. It's revealed in His grace and sacrifice. We believe in the doctrinal truth and unity of faith, not differing from its teachings and standards. Unity of the faith and spirit is maintained and perfected by accepting the message of the Old Testament prophets and the New Testament apostles. Thereby we continue growing in grace, advancing toward spiritual maturity, and are filled with all the fullness of Jesus Christ. The existence of one faith is expressed by our actions, because not having a demonstration of our faith and trust in God shows that we have no part in Him. One faith preserves our loyalty to Jesus Christ, contending with the adversaries of the gospel, because God has called us to stand firm in the faith, letting nothing move or destroy our ministry. Importantly, followers of Christ must always share in the same faith and experience, the same baptism of the Holy Spirit of Christ, to be in oneness.

There is only one baptism, which is the initiation into Christ's body. This can only be accomplished by the Holy Spirit of Christ, the instrument used by God to baptize believers. There are two types of baptism mentioned in the Holy Scriptures—physical baptism, which is of water, and spiritual baptism, which is of the spirit. Water baptism symbolizes the death and resurrection of Jesus Christ, where the believer is dead to sin and is raised with Christ. Immersion in the water signifies the cleansing of our heart and the washing away of our sins by the blood of Jesus Christ. Baptism of repentance by water was the instrument John the Baptist used to baptize people; however, he prophesied that Jesus Christ, who is greater than he, would baptize with the Holy Spirit. Water baptism is publicly aligning ourselves

111

with Christ. It is important to know that water baptism can save a person once he or she has genuinely repented (Mark 1:8, John 3:5).

Spiritual baptism takes place when God pours out His spirit upon an individual to empower him or her for His service and ministry on earth, as seen on the day of Pentecost. This baptism is a sign and dynamic mark of a true follower of Christ. Each baptism is an act of obedience after faith. It is a part of our rejection of sin, our commitment to Christ and His Will, resulting in a continual flow of grace and divine life to us, thus reflecting God's standards of righteousness. Hence, Jesus Christ commanded His disciples not to witness until they were endowed with the power from on high, which is the Holy Spirit. The disciples were saved according to the Old Testament covenant provisions. They were not regenerated in the full new covenant until they entered the new covenant based on Jesus's death and resurrection, which they received on the day of Pentecost, being baptized with the Holy Spirit of Christ. The word *baptism* refers to submerging or immersing. It implies that a change has taken place in a person's life (Acts 1:4–8, 2:4).

Benefits of one baptism include the following:

- It actualizes our crucifixion with Christ
- It is our initiation in the spirit's fullness
- It is our separation from the powers of sin
- It is the basis for keeping unity in the church
- It joins us to the body of Christ

It is important for us not to be confused with the filling of the Holy Spirit and the baptism of the Holy Spirit, for they are two distinct works of the spirit that are often separated by time. The filling of the Holy Spirit is received at regeneration when a person repents, accepts Jesus Christ, and is baptized in the name of Jesus Christ. That person becomes a new creation in Christ, a child of God, where he or she is no longer conformed to the world. The baptism of the Holy Spirit is the supernatural gift of God's power given to His followers to empower us to witness for Him in power and be of service to Him in our ministries. Baptism of the Holy Spirit only occurs once in a believer's life. This baptism of the Holy Spirit brings boldness and the power of the spirit into the lives of all followers of Christ so they can accomplish mighty works for God and make their witness and proclamation effective. Notably, Jesus Himself did not enter His ministry until He had been baptized with the Holy Spirit after He was baptized by John the Baptist in the River Jordon (Acts 10:37–43, Luke 4:18).

The final element of oneness is "One God and Father of all." The holy scriptures tell us emphatically that there is only one God, He alone is God, and He has no help in creation, for there is none worthy to be praised but Him alone. God is a spirit. He has no beginning or ending. God the Father always was, always has been, and always will be. He is holy. He is eternal and everlasting. Moreover, He has no mother or father. He is the Almighty God. He made the heavens by His power. He established the world by His wisdom and stretched the heavens by His understanding. The purpose of one God is that all humanity will know Him as the true and living God, for there is no limitation to Him. He is infallible and the creator of all things. He is perfection, and He cannot die. He is a God of His word, actions, and deeds, and there is no one equal to Him, for He alone can forgive the sins of this world (Deuteronomy 6:4, John 4:24).

God is revealed in the scripture as an infinite, eternal, self-existent being, who is the first cause of all that is, for He is from everlasting to everlasting. God revealed Himself to the people of Israel as one God to worship. He appeared to Moses in the burning bush and addressed Himself as the God of his fathers, Abraham, Isaac, and Jacob. Moses asked God, "When I go the children of Israel, whom should I say sent me?" God responded, "Tell them I Am That I Am sent thee." God gave Himself a personal name: "I Am That I Am," which is the Hebrew name "Yahweh," indicating that He is to be known as the God who is present and active. This name Yahweh expresses God's faithfulness, love, and care for His children, and He lives in fellowship with us, which corresponds with the fundamental promise of the covenant to be God (Exodus 3:14).

A description of God's oneness includes the following:

- There is no god after Him
- There is no god besides Him
- There is no god before Him
- There is no god equal to Him
- There is no god greater than Him
- There is no god with Him

The prophets of the Old Testament, Jesus Christ, and the apostles all recognize God as one. The four beasts worshipped one God, and the Apostle John saw only one God sitting on the throne in heaven. There is one God to us, His people—the Father of whom all things are made—and we are in Him. God

Himself attests to His oneness as He said in His Word, "I, even I, am He and there is no god with me"(Deuteronomy 32:39-40). He further tells us, "I lift up my hand to heaven and say I live for ever" (Deuteronomy 39:40). God's oneness serves as the basis that prohibits the worshiping of other gods; rather, we are commanded to fear Him and serve only Him. God is all powerful among all the gods and spirits of this world, for He is all knowing and does not need any help. He is omnipresent, omnipotent, and omniscient; therefore, He must be the sole object of our love and obedience (Revelation 4:1–8,).

The worshiping of one God makes the Christian faith unique, because only God the Father was before time, and He created all things. His spirit rules on the earth, in the hearts of and among His people as they hunger and thirst for His presence and power in their lives. He existed eternally and infinitely before creating the universe and is independent of and prior to all that has been created in heaven and on earth. God the Father is different and independent from His creation, whether humans, angels, spirits, physical or material things. His Being and His existence are in a totally different realm, for He dwells in perfect, pure existence far above others and His creation. God is powerful, for He transcends all other gods of this world.

Some attributes of God the Father include the following:

- He is good
- He is holy
- He is immutable and unchanging
- He is infinitely wise
- He is love

- He is merciful
- He is omnipotent
- He is omnipresent
- He is omniscient
- He is self-existing
- He is sovereign
- He is transcendent

God the Father is eternal; He is a spirit by nature with no beginning. His existence will never end, for He is immortal and infinite. The scripture tells us, "Before the mountain was brought forth and the earth formed God was from everlasting to everlasting" (Psalms 90:2). He and the scripture attest to it as we read, "In the beginning God created the heavens and the earth," which signifies that He was before all things. God is uncreated, unoriginated, He owes no one for His existence but Himself; hence, Jesus Christ tells us that "God the Father has life in Himself"(John 5:26). God is incomparable; there is none like Him in the heavens or under the heavens. God is one, being perfect, pure, and just. He is one in nature and essence. He is the consuming fire worthy of our worship, praise, and devotion, for He alone sits in heaven on the throne with all power and authority.

The doctrine of "one God" focuses on the idea of the Almighty and Powerful God for His people to learn His ways and to be introduced to the intelligence of God. The scripture tells us that things about God were not written for we would not be able to comprehend them, and the secret things belong to God. He makes known to us that which He wants us to know to follow His law. The formation of man represents the existence of "one God"; thus God says, "I make man in my image." One Adam represents one image. Adam took on the name of the first father because he was the first man as he took on the reflection of God. Moreover, He created one man, indicating there is one God. In the giving of the Ten Commandments, it begins with an emphasis on the oneness of God; furthermore, God revealed Himself as the only one to be worshiped (Genesis 1:26–27).

God is a supreme Being and ruler over the heavens and the earth; therefore, the focus of our worship ultimately must go to God the Father of all things. Both the physical and spiritual comes from Him, and He must be the first and the highest priority in the hearts and minds of mankind. He is the greatest. He existed before time. He brought time and life into existence. Nothing was before Him and at the end of this life, we all will see Him face to face as the only one true, living God. All nations, kindred, and people shall bow and worship Him as the Almighty God, the everlasting Father.

My Testimony of Trials and Tribulations

The year 2020 was the most difficult time of my entire life. It is a year I will always remember.

Writing this book was very challenging and difficult for me; however, it was a source of strength and relief for my broken heart and spirit. Prior to this, I thought that my life was perfect. I was living a holy and godly life, having no cares in this world. I felt that everything was good and wonderful with me, for I was solid in my relationship with God, and nothing could have shaken it or gotten between God and me. So, I thought.

I was so wrong. While on vacation in the Caribbean in 2019, I met a good friend of mine again, someone whom I loved secretly for some years prior to me migrating overseas. After our reconnection as friends, we got close again, and eventually I sinned against God and my body by committing fornication after five years of abstinence. Although I knew it was wrong, I allowed myself to continue in that sin. After returning home, I continued having a long-distance relationship with this man. While in the Caribbean, I saw a glimpse of his behavior but brushed it off, and during the long-distance relationship, the situation became very toxic, as he would verbally abuse me over the phone, yet I continued with this man. In January 2020, I hesitantly went back to the Caribbean, and then I got the full brunt of his verbal abuse. I had never experienced such in my life before. It was horrible, yet I stayed with him, although my family told me to end the relationship. I held on because of my love for this man. He would rain verbal abuse on me, yet I stayed and showed him love, hoping that he would change but to no avail. At times, when in a good mood, he would apologize, but the next day or thereabout, he would continue his usual ways with his verbal abuse. I stayed in that abusive condition for two months, until eventually, I found the courage to end the relationship. I then caught the next available flight out of the Caribbean and returned to my place of residence.

Shortly after coming home, I found out that I had lost my job because I had overstayed on my vacation and did not inform my place of work. So now I was heartbroken and had no work, wow! My life at that moment was in a mess, but although the pain was so fresh, deep, and painful, I realized that God alone could help me. So, I refocused my mind back on God, and in agony and pain, I cried out to Him with sincere repentance, seeking His forgiveness, thereby rededicating and submitting my entire life back to Him. Shortly thereafter, I immediately got my manuscript and began typing out the content of this book. Tears were falling constantly on the computer keyboard as I typed, and thoughts of my failed relationship came into my mind to distract me. Somehow, I gain the courage to continue by focusing on God and the book and not on the hurt and pain

I was enduring. As days turned into weeks and weeks into months, I became stronger and stronger, especially because I could sense and feel God's presence penetrating my life through each word in this book, which ultimately gave me the strength I needed to persevere. God's Word is true, for the scripture says, "He healeth the broken hearted, and bindeth up their wounds"(Psalm 147:3). For me, God has been faithful in the healing process of my life and heart for He continues to strengthen me so that I can accomplish His will in my life.

As I began to recover, I was speaking to a family member on the phone who told me that my grandmother along with one of my uncles told her that I was the one responsible for beating up my mother years ago, but the truth was it was my older sister, their favorite, who committed that assault. It was that same lie I had cried over for years constantly because it was the most hurtful and painful lie out of all my mother's lies that she told about me, for it destroyed my entire life. That lie my mother used to discredit and tarnish my reputation, as people looked at me and called me a curse and an evil child. Now hearing such from that family member hurt me even more, as I was not expecting those two people to repeat such a blatant lie, for both were present at the time of the incident. My grandmother that night accompanied my sister and the police to the station. It is so painful to see how evil, vindictive, and wicked your own family can be. Yes, my family treated me wickedly, but to hear this? Wow! I know that they don't love me and will never, but, my God, how wicked can a person be, knowing the truth and putting the blame on me? Wow! I often cry bitterly about that lie in front of my children and their father, but that day in April, I cried so much my heart was beating fast, my head started hurting, and I couldn't catch my breath as I was hyperventilating in agony. Then my daughters began to cry and embrace me, and my son came and hugged me, trying to calm me down. Eventually they succeeded in calming me down. Then I called Sonia, my friend, and told her what had happened. She said to me, "Correna, you need to put those hurts in God's hands and leave them there. You have been taking it back from God. You need to give those burdens to God and leave them with Him." She said to me, "Cast all our burdens upon the Lord, and He shall sustain thee; He shall never suffer the righteous to be moved." That night, I cried out to God in pain and agony about all that I had endured because of those lies that were told on me by my mother and my family members—the wickedness, evil, and abandonment from my family—the suffering and hardships I'd encountered from them—and gave them to God. After that prayer, I felt such a relief and calmness, thus ending a life of crying, pain, and suffering that was caused by my mother and her lies. I then sought the help of a professional counselor to help me heal from all that pain, suffering, abandonment, neglect, and lack of love I experienced from the age of four to the present. The counseling helped me dramatically, as I realized that there were people I had to forgive, including my ex-boyfriend. Forgiveness is one of the most important keys to healing. After all that had transpired in my life to this point, I now realized that the heartbreak was a blessing for me. I thank God for putting my ex-boyfriend in my life to bring me to such a low point and making me realize I needed healing not only from this heartbreak but from all those hurtful experiences I had endured all my life. Looking back on what transpired in my life, I realized that God could not have used me in the state that I was in prior to me falling into sin. Yes, I was right with God spiritually; however, for God to fulfil His plan and purpose in my life, He had to break me because of the unresolved issues, pain, suffering, and hurt I endured, stemming from my childhood to the present. All my life, I had cried in pain and suffered because of those lies; however, this April was the last time that I broke down and cried because of those lies.

At this present stage in my life, God is putting me through the refinery process, where He is healing me emotionally, mentally, physically, and spiritually so that He can mold and shape me into the vessel that He can use for His glory. The God I serve is amazing, for He is sovereign, good, and loving. He allowed me to be at home where I could finish typing this book and heal, thereby showing me that His grace is sufficient. Within a month, I got my job back. My life was now heading in the right direction. I had healed from my past pains and my heartbreak and was back to work, so I thought. I experienced the biggest shock of my life months after when a large lump came up under my right armpit. I went to my general practitioner, who then examined it and referred me to the breast care unit on an urgent basis to have the lump looked at. A mammogram was done and a biopsy sample taken to be tested for cancer. On September 4, 2020, three days after my birthday, I got the diagnosis: "Your results show cancer."

I was expecting to hear the diagnosis, so I was very calm as the doctor told me. My mind went blank, and all that came to my head was *I have to trust God.* That was repeating in my head as the doctor spoke to me. The doctor asked me, "How do you feel?"

I said nothing. She then continued to tell me how sorry she was that she couldn't give me better news, but all that was in my head was *I have to trust God.* She then asked if I had any questions. I just shook my head no, and then the only words that came out of my mouth were "I have to trust God."

The doctor said to me, "You are taking it very well," and gave me my paperwork.

I drove home without a tear in my eyes because I knew all I had to do was to trust God. I am a strong woman of God, and I see how God has brought me through many trials in my life. I came home and told my daughters the news. One of them started crying. I said to her, "Stop crying. Do not give the devil something to gloat about." I comforted her and told her I would be all right. I said to her, "Cancer killed many of my family members on my father's side, but it will not kill me." Then I got myself ready and went to off to work one hour later.

When I came home from work after 10:00 p.m. that night, my son was so happy to see Mommy as usual. I said to him, "I have something to tell you," but he was still playing around. Then I shouted to him, "I have cancer." I heard my son scream. Then he held his heart and braced himself to the wall. I was so scared because I thought he was going to have a heart attack, so I went and held him. He put his head on my shoulder because he couldn't stand up still. He looked different, and I was so frightened. As I held him, I called a friend who is nurse and explained what had happened. She told me that he was in shock and to take him for a walk. He looked weak. I was afraid of letting him lie down, so we walked around the neighborhood. Still, I had to hold him, as he could not balance himself. After about fifteen minutes of walking, he came back to himself and told me after I told him the diagnosis, he felt a sharp pain in his heart, and he blacked out.

I was diagnosed with *triple negative cancer*, one of the most aggressive and lethal types of breast cancer. It is the hardest to treat and is not curable. In my case, the doctors do not know where the cancer came from, but they are suspecting it is from the breast, as it was in my armpit, and normally when that happens, it comes from the breast, although nothing was found in the breast. My doctor then discussed treatments. She wanted me to do chemotherapy because of the type of cancer that I had and because my body tested negative for hormonal or targeted therapy treatments that could help me. I told the doctor plainly that I would not take chemotherapy, and I trusted in my God that He would heal me. As I continued to visit the hospital, the doctors tried to convince me to have chemo, as it was my only hope of surviving this cancer, yet I stood my ground, saying no to chemo. I told the doctors that I trusted in the power of God and my faith in Him, and I believed that He would heal me. I had so many doctors trying to convince me. At one point, there were three doctors together telling me to take chemo, and they brought all types of science to me. One doctor said to me, "I know you have faith, and it's good to have faith, but we know what's best for you because we believe in science and what it says about your cancer."

I turned to the doctor and said, "You may believe in science, but I believe in the God, who created science. He will heal me." After that meeting, in October, after going back and forth with the doctors, they wanted me to run other tests. They were pressuring me. That meeting lasted over an hour so I gave in and said that I would do the test. I was not happy after agreeing, so I told my children I would pray about it. That night, I did, and the next morning, I said, "I will not do any other tests because I will make things worse for me, as the cancer will spread more in my body." That day, God was leading me as I tried calling the doctor and couldn't get the doctor, so I left a voice message on one of the nurse's lines. While I washed dishes, the Holy Spirit said to me, "Correna, you're not sure if that nurse will get the message. Remember, they gave you a card to call them directly," so I ran and looked for the card. I called, and immediately, I heard a voice on the other line. I advised her to tell the doctors I would no longer go to London for further tests. I wanted to proceed with the surgery. I then advised I had left the same message on a particular nurse's phone, only for her to tell me the nurse was on leave. I told her to tell the doctors that I wanted to have the surgery and then radiotherapy. Again, they continued to remind me that neither surgery nor radiotherapy would cure me. Anyway, within days of that call, the doctor's office called me, telling me they had to squeeze me in between two patients so that I could get an appointment date for the surgery, but again, they were sure to remind me that the surgery would not cure me. Now, tell me if God is not good; it's always good to follow the leadings of the Holy Spirit.

The following week, on November 12, 2020, I had surgery. However, before the surgery, my doctor told me it would not cure me, and if I wanted to change my mind, I could simply say no. After the surgery, the doctor told me she took out five lymph nodes that were cancerous; however, she did not get all and had to leave one cancerous lymph node that was stuck onto my blood vessel. Weeks before I started radiotherapy, I received a call from my general practitioner, who told me that he had heard I had the surgery and I wanted to do radiotherapy. He then proceeded to tell me as the other doctors did so many times that radiotherapy would not heal me and began telling me that chemo was my best hope of surviving this cancer. I said to my general practitioner, "I am not taking chemo, and if it is God's will for me to live or die. Whichever way God chooses, I am fine with, either way."

Then he said to me, "All right," and quickly ended the call. After the call, I began to cry and said to my children, "These doctors believe that the only thing that can cure me is chemo. It's like they are saying chemo is bigger than my God. It really makes me mad to see that they believe so much in chemo and not the power of God."

Before I began my radiotherapy, I received another call from my cancer doctor, telling me again that the radiotherapy would not cure me. For them, my only hope of a cure was chemotherapy. From the beginning of this trying period in my life, I trusted God completely, and my faith remains steadfast in Him. Throughout this trial, I knew that I would not die because I knew that God had a plan for my life. I was in the beginning stage of His plan, and He was not through with me. Hence, I continued to trust God and let His will be done in my life, no matter what. I will say like Job "though he slay me, yet will I trust Him" (Job 13:15). I started three weeks of radiotherapy treatment on January 6, 2021 and finished February 2021. I had a follow-up appointment with the doctor and requested that I get another CT scan to prove to those doctors that my God is a miracle-working God because I knew that I was healed from cancer. On March 19, 2021, I had the scan, and on April 21, 2021, I got the results, which showed no trace of cancer in my body. The doctor couldn't believe the result and requested for me to do another CT scan in a few months' time to make sure that the cancer did not come back. I told him right then and there that the cancer would not come back because I was healed by God, and when He heals, He heals completely. On July 26, 2021, I had my second CT scan done, and on August 18, 2021, the results showed that I am cancer free again with no sign of any reoccurrence. Yet still, the doctors cannot believe it. They are baffled at the results, so again, they requested for me to do another scan in another six months. To those doctors, it's unreal to see such healing take place in an incurable situation such as mine, but what they fail to realize is that I serve a God of the impossibilities, and absolutely nothing is too hard for Him. To God be the glory for the great things He has done. I am so grateful and thankful to God for His miraculous healing in my life, proving to those doctors who are Hindus and Muslim that I worship the true and living God and the mighty healer. I am grateful and thankful to God that throughout this process, His glory was shown in and through me, by my faith in Him. The doctors and nurses now know that the true and living God is all powerful and mighty. Glory be to God, who never forsakes His children. I can unequivocally say that God is a miracle-working God, and He still heals, even in these times. Throughout this process, I never wavered in my belief in God. Instead, I continued to work in His vineyard by teaching His Word on a podcast, witnessing to nurses and drivers who took me to my treatments, trying to win as many souls as possible for the kingdom of God. I never slowed down in doing the work of God even while battling this cancer because my eyes were not on the cancer. Rather they were on God, the solution to all my problems.

To those who may be facing difficulties in life, don't give up. I know that at times it's hard, especially when you experience pain, suffering, and life-threatening situations, but do as I did, which was to immerse myself in God and His Word, for that was and is my source of strength. Then stand firm in God, His Word, and His promises, and have confidence in the God that you serve, knowing that He will surely make a way of escape for you. Blessings.

My life is in God's hands, and my hope is built on nothing less than Jesus Christ and His righteousness.

I cannot say that this process in my life was easy because it was not. It was one of the hardest things I had to go undergo. However, I placed my trust and faith in God and focused on the task ahead. Today, the book is published, and it will bless and change lives and lead people to God.

Special Note

This book is to show that God can use a person who has been looked down on, lied on, and abandoned and who has fallen and been broken to accomplish His purpose in this world.

All praise and glory be unto God!

The Invitation to Christ

To surrender your life to God and be saved, here is what you must do:

1. Repent of your sins.
2. Believe and accept Jesus Christ as your savior.
3. Be baptized in the name of Jesus Christ.
4. Pray and wait for the baptism of the Holy Ghost.

I implore you to find a Christ-centered church that preaches the true gospel of Christ and fellowship with them. Strive to live a holy life pleasing unto God.

Welcome to the family of Christ.

Printed and bound by CPI Group (UK) Ltd, Croydon, CR0 4YY